Should I Try to Work It Out?

A Guidebook for Individuals and Couples

at the Crossroads of Divorce

Alan J. Hawkins, Ph.D., Tamara Fackrell, J.D., Ph.D.,

& Steven M. Harris, Ph.D., MFT

© 2013 All rights reserved.
ISBN: 978-1491228975

CONTENTS

TITLE	PAGE

vi   Contents

Chapter 1

Introduction and Overview

Divorce is such a gut-wrenching experience, and there isn't anyone I know that hasn't come through it without their whole world just turned upside down.

Janet,[*] divorced, single mom

The day my parents got divorced was the happiest day of my life. They got out of a bad marriage and began focusing on being better parents.

Amanda, 20-year-old college student

Overview: In this chapter you will learn about the general purpose of this guidebook. It is designed to be a resource to individuals at the crossroads of divorce; that is, for individuals who are thinking about divorce or whose spouse is thinking about divorce. Divorce is a very personal matter but it is also a serious public issue because of the costs to taxpayers of divorce. So for both public and private reasons, you and your children deserve nothing less than careful consideration of whether divorce is the right thing to do and to make that decision based on the best information possible.

❖ James and Shelly were considering divorce. They have three children. Shelly wanted to divorce, but James wanted to save the marriage. Shelly had a long list of issues that the couple needed to work on. She had rarely been open about her disappointment in their marriage, but there had been a few frank conversations over the years. As with many couples who divorce, the tension escalated and they had a big fight. Shelly took the children an hour away from her home to her mother's house. She wanted to think carefully about her options as she decided how to proceed.

❖ Hilary and Sam had come to a crossroads in their marriage. Hilary was an alcoholic and the couple had many marital problems that arose out of the addiction. Sam decided he was

---

[*] All names have been changed to protect privacy.

ready to move on and divorce. Hilary wanted to work through the marital issues. She promised that this time, she would get her addiction in check. This was a second marriage for both of them and they each had children from their previous marriages, as well as children together from the current marriage.

❖ Felicia and Rolando were also at the crossroads of divorce. Felicia had yelled about an issue regarding their children. Rolando had stayed calm, but Felicia was heartbroken and refused to talk about the problem. As occurs with some couples, the couple separated abruptly and had avoided trying to work it out. Felicia took the children with her. They needed to decide if this separation was going to become a permanent fixture in their lives.

This guidebook is a way to help couples like Sam and Hilary, James and Shelly, and Felicia and Rolando make important choices that come up when a couple is deciding between working through marital problems or divorcing.

A. What is the purpose of this guidebook?

This guidebook is designed to be a resource to individuals who may be thinking about getting a divorce or whose spouse is thinking about divorce. These individuals are at the "crossroads of divorce," facing a challenging decision that has powerful consequences for the future of their own lives, the lives of family members, and their communities. This guidebook contains research-based information about important questions that individuals at the crossroads of divorce often have, such as:

❖ Can my marriage be repaired and can we be happy again?

❖ Is divorce a reliable path to happiness?

❖ What are the effects of divorce on children, adults, and the communities they live in?

❖ What can I expect will happen during the legal process of getting a divorce? What are the legal options for ending a marriage?

We try to answer these kinds of questions and many more in this guidebook.

We know that these are sensitive and difficult questions to answer. Circumstances are different for everyone. We believe that divorce is a solution that many people consider in order to restore health and happiness to their lives; it is one method of dealing with marital struggles and trials. Further, we believe there are valid reasons for a divorce. And many individuals going through divorce want to keep working to save the marriage but their partners do not. The law allows one partner to end a marriage without the consent of his or her spouse. We try in this guidebook to be sensitive to different situations. It is not our intention to make judgments about what individuals should or should not do in difficult, personal circumstances.

At the same time, we try to present the scientific research on marriage and divorce accurately and fairly. And the research is clear that, in general, the process of family breakup marked by divorce has potential problems for children, adults, and the communities they live in. In some instances, divorce actually improves the lives of those involved, but for the most part, researchers have found that divorce generally puts children at two to three times the risk for a wide range of negative effects. And it is hard on adults, as well. Research also suggests that some individuals at the crossroads of divorce may be able to repair their marriages and avoid those potential negative consequences. A lot of good research identifies the knowledge and skills that individuals need to form and sustain a healthy and happy marriage. And there are good resources available to help those who want to work to keep trying to improve their relationship. If you decide to divorce, there are legal options to consider that may be better for you and your children. This guidebook can give you solid information that will help you make the best choices in your individual circumstances. It's not a "how-to" book to fix problems in your marriage, although we suggest some resources that you could access to get some of that kind of help. The book is about providing you with as much information as possible about the realities of divorce so you can make the best decision possible for your situation. We hope this book will help you choose the right path forward—to divorce or to keep trying to work it out.

Brittany, a divorced single mother whom we once interviewed, shared with us her strong personal feelings about the need for better education to help people make decisions about divorce:

> What would I share with those who are approaching the decision of divorce? Explore every single avenue possible. … I think that it should be required that they go to a full-day, 8-hour course on "this is what happens [with divorce], this is

how many days you get [with your kids], these are the holidays you get, this is how many days a year you get to see them. This is how this works." ... I truly think that people start the process [of divorce] but they don't know what the ramifications are, but once they find out what the ramifications are, they are in it so far that they don't want to go backwards. So if they knew up front how it was going to work and what would happen to the kids, and the cost, I think people would be more apt to try harder. I think it should be required that they go to a course before they even file [for divorce].

Most states these days require that divorcing parents (with dependent children) take a brief class to help them be good co-parents to their children after the divorce and help their children adjust to the divorce[1]; research suggests that these classes help improve outcomes for children and adults.[2] In addition to helping parents understand some of the potential effects of divorce for their children and helping them learn ways to minimize negative effects, some of these required classes raise the issue of potential reconciliation. A few states now require or are considering a requirement that issues around reconciliation be a significant part of these classes.[3] If you live in a state with this kind of requirement, this guidebook would be an excellent supplement to the class.

We hope this *Crossroads of Divorce* guidebook can be useful to people in other circumstances, as well. For instance, individuals who may not be thinking too seriously about divorce but are experiencing the struggles and disappointments that almost all married couples face could be motivated to work to improve their relationship to avoid the challenges of divorce. Some may be thinking more seriously about divorce but haven't taken any formal steps in that direction. This guidebook can be a valuable source of information for those individuals, too. Sometimes family members and friends who are watching loved ones struggle with their marriages want valid information, like the information in this guidebook, to share with loved ones. In addition, perhaps the information in this guidebook can help those who have already experienced a divorce understand some of the challenges they have faced and better prepare for future relationships. Marriage counselors, religious leaders, lawyers, and mediators who are working with couples facing a possible divorce may want to recommend use of this guidebook. Many couples these days are not married but have been living together for some time and have children together. We think many of the issues that these couples face when deciding to break up or stay together are similar to those married couples face. So we think this book can be valuable for them, as well. And because most people think that divorce is a serious problem in our society, this guidebook has general educational value; it is not limited just to those who are currently facing the potential breakdown of their marriage.

Using This Guidebook. There is a lot of information in this guidebook. You may be more interested in some parts and less interested in others. We don't assume you will read the entire guidebook cover to cover, so there may be some repetition of information in the various chapters. Select the parts that are most helpful to you. You may want to look over the table of contents to see which parts might be most helpful. Brief overviews are at the beginning of each chapter. In addition to all the research-based information that is presented, sprinkled throughout the guidebook are stories and quotations from real people we have interviewed who have been at the crossroads of divorce, telling how they handled their challenges, what they decided to do, and how things have worked out for them. Stories like these put a more human face on the difficult topic of repairing a marriage or getting a divorce than you are likely to get from all the research findings we present. (We have changed the names of these individuals to preserve their privacy.)

Also, at the end of each chapter, there are some writing exercises or self-guided activities so that you can evaluate your own situation and think about your best course of action. We think these exercises are one of the most valuable parts of the guidebook. Sometimes people at the crossroads of divorce can be caught up in emotions; it can be difficult to sort out thoughts and feelings. Moreover, they often lack helpful information about marriage and divorce. In these situations, people often make decisions that satisfy them for the short run but may not be the best decision for the long run. If you take the time to do these exercises, they may help you think more clearly about your decision. We encourage you to do Exercise 1.1, "Plan Your Use of This Guidebook," at the end of this chapter. It will help you get an overview of the guidebook and encourage you to plan your use of it.

B. Why should we be concerned about the divorce rate? Isn't it just a personal and private matter?

Most people these days think that high divorce rates are a serious problem in our society.[4] And as we mentioned earlier, many states these days require parents to attend a divorcing parents class. Some states include in the class information about working through problems and avoiding divorce, if possible. Why should policy makers care about this? Aren't these just personal matters? The answer to this question is that the decision to divorce is both a highly personal matter but also an important public issue. Many children's lives are negatively affected by family breakdown and policy makers want to minimize harm to children. Each year about 1 million children experience the divorce of their parents.[5] Moreover, divorce has financial impact not only on the families that go through it but also on all taxpaying citizens. Divorce is one of the leading reasons that children (and adults, especially women) fall into poverty. When this happens, the state has various programs that provide temporary assistance. These programs are expensive. One national study conservatively estimated the cost nationwide of family fragmentation—divorce and having children without marrying—to be $112 billion a year.[6] Another study estimated the cost of divorce to taxpayers in Texas to be more than $3 billion a year, which represents one out of every eight dollars of the Texas state budget.[7] And these numbers don't even take into consideration the personal costs to families to pay for the divorce and set up two different households after the divorce is finalized.

After careful consideration, if some marriages can be repaired and families remain intact, then everyone probably is better off: the children, the parents, and their taxpaying neighbors. If individuals choose a divorce, then it is important for them to be well informed of what to expect, what legal options are available, and what they can do to help their children adjust well to the changes. A "good" divorce is also better for children, adults, and government budgets.

So for both public and private reasons, we believe that you and your children deserve nothing less than careful consideration of whether divorce is the right thing to do and to make that decision based on the best information possible. We encourage you to take the time to review the information and do the exercises in this guidebook. Whatever your decision, we wish you and your family the best as you weigh your options and seek clarity and confidence in your decision making about your marriage.

Like James and Shelly, in the example at the beginning of the chapter, you may decide that counseling will help you make a more sound decision. James attended counseling on his own to help him work through some personal issues that had contributed to his marital problems. James and Shelly ultimately decided to stay together and over time rebuilt a happy marriage. Or, like Hilary and Sam, you may decide to divorce and carefully consider your options of how best to proceed. Hilary and Sam used the divorce mediation process to amicably resolve some of the main issues they experienced in their marriage, but ultimately decided to divorce. They continued to work at being effective co-parents for the sake of their children. We hope you won't be like Felicia and Rolando, whose emotions drove them almost unthinkingly toward divorce, blocking any communication with each other and preventing any attempt to salvage civility in the relationship even though they will continue to be involved with each other as co-parents to their children for the rest of their lives. They fought an expensive battle in court and the litigation over the children continued as each of them remarried.

Exercise for Chapter 1

1.1: Plan Your Use of this Guidebook

Often it is a good idea to start an activity with a goal and a plan. We invite you to do that for this guidebook. First, we suggest you look over the table of contents to get a better idea of the specific topics included in the guidebook. The various chapters and sections of each chapter are titled with a question that people at the crossroads of divorce often have. Next, you may want to skim the overview at the beginning of each chapter to see if it is something you are interested in. Then think about how valuable the information in the chapter will be to you. If you believe it will be valuable, make a plan to go over the material and complete some of the activities.

Using the guidelines below, for each chapter indicate how important you think the information will be to you (circle the number for your answer). Then, indicate when you would like to have read the material and completed some or all the activities. Please consider carefully; make this a contract with yourself to help you think clearly at this challenging crossroad in your life.

Then, after doing this, pause for a moment and think about your overall goal for this guidebook. Perhaps you seriously want to think about working more on your relationship and avoiding divorce, so your goal may be to find ways to do this. Perhaps you don't have much choice—the divorce is being forced on you—so maybe your goal is to make this transition as easy as possible for your children. Whatever your goal might be, write it down.

Chapter 2: Can unhappy marriages become happy again? How?				
How important do you think this chapter will be to you?	1 Not Important	2 Somewhat Important	3 Pretty Important	4 Very Important
When will you read it and work on the activities?			Finish date goal:	

Chapter 3: How common is divorce and what are the reasons?				
How important do you think this chapter will be to you?	1 Not Important	2 Somewhat Important	3 Pretty Important	4 Very Important
When will you read it and work on the activities?			Finish date goal:	

Chapter 4: Does divorce help adults become happier?				
How important do you think this chapter will be to you?	1 Not Important	2 Somewhat Important	3 Pretty Important	4 Very Important
When will you read it and work on the activities?			Finish date goal:	

Chapter 5: What are the possible consequences of divorce for children?				
How important do you think this chapter will be to you?	1 Not Important	2 Somewhat Important	3 Pretty Important	4 Very Important
When will you read it and work on the activities?			Finish date goal:	

Chapter 6: What are the possible consequences of divorce for adults?				
How important do you think this chapter will be to you?	1 Not Important	2 Somewhat Important	3 Pretty Important	4 Very Important
When will you read it and work on the activities?			Finish date goal:	

Chapter 7: What are the financial consequences of divorce?				
How important do you think this chapter will be to you?	1 Not Important	2 Somewhat Important	3 Pretty Important	4 Very Important
When will you read it and work on the activities?			Finish date goal:	

Chapter 8: What are the legal options for divorce? What should I expect during the divorce process?				
How important do you think this chapter will be to you?	1 Not Important	2 Somewhat Important	3 Pretty Important	4 Very Important
When will you read it and work on the activities?			Finish date goal:	

Now write down your overall goal for your use of this guidebook:

_____

_____

_____

_____

[1] Pollet, S. L., & Lombreglia, M. (2008). A nationwide survey of mandatory parent education. *Family Court Review, 46,* 375–394.

[2] Fackrell, T. A., Hawkins, A. J., & Kay, N. M. (2011). How effective are court-affiliated divorcing parents education programs? A meta-analytic study. *Family Court Review, 49,* 107–119.

[3] Since 2007, Utah has required a 1-hour divorce orientation class in conjunction with the mandated divorcing parents class. The purpose of the class is to help individuals considering a divorce think carefully about their options, including repairing problems in the marriage and keeping a family together, and to inform individuals of the potential consequences of divorce. The class also informs people of their legal options for divorce. As of spring 2013, several other states were considering requiring similar classes focused on the potential for reconciliation (e.g., Georgia, North Carolina, Oklahoma, Texas). See divorcereform.us

[4] See Schramm, D. G., Marshall, J. P., Harris, V. W., & George, A. (2003). *Marriage in Utah: 2003 baseline statewide survey on marriage and divorce.* Salt Lake City: Utah Department of Workforce Services (see p. 19). See also *With this ring ... A national survey on marriage in America.* Gaithersburg, MD: National Fatherhood Initiative (see p. 29).

[5] National Center for Health Statistics. (2008). *Marriage and divorce.* Available at: www.cdc.gov/nchs/fastats/divorce.htm

[6] Scafidi, B. (2008). *The taxpayer costs of divorce and unwed childbearing: First-ever estimates for the nation and all fifty states.* New York: Institute for American Values.

[7] Schramm, D. G., Harris, S. M., Whiting, J., Hawkins, A. J., Brown, M., & Porter, R. (2013). Economic costs and policy implications associated with divorce: Texas as a case study. *Journal of Divorce and Remarriage, 54,* 1–24.

Chapter 2

Can Unhappy Marriages
Become Happy Again? How?

One advantage of marriage, it seems to me, is that when you fall out of love with each other, it keeps you together until maybe you fall in again.

Judith Viorst, American author and journalist[1]

I think a man and a woman should choose each other for life, for the simple reason that a long life with all its accidents is barely enough for a man and a woman to understand each other; and in this case to understand is to love.

William Butler Yeats[2]

Overview: Most unhappy marriages become happy again, if couples can stick it out through the hard times. While some divorces are necessary, some marriages can be repaired. Some individuals and couples read books or use other resources on their own to help improve their marriages. Others participate in marriage education classes to improve their relationship skills; some resources for finding good marriage education classes are reviewed here. Still others seek counseling from professional counselors or therapists, or seek help from a trusted religious guide. This chapter contains some useful guidelines for choosing a good counselor or therapist to help you repair your marriage. Through dedicated efforts, some couples are able to reconcile and rebuild a happy marriage. Even if your spouse doesn't seem to be interested in working out problems in the marriage, there are things you can do individually that may repair your relationship. Ten characteristics of a healthy marriage are discussed.

Some may be surprised to learn that many unhappy marriages recover. As one respected marriage therapist and researcher, Dr. William J. Doherty at the University of Minnesota, noted, marriages are *not* like fruit. When fruit gets bruised or rotten, it doesn't improve with time; you just have to toss it out. Marriages, however, often do improve over time. Nationally, about one in seven (13%) married individuals say that they have seriously thought about divorcing their spouse recently.[3] But more than 94% of married individuals—both men and women—who said that their marriage at some point was in trouble said they were glad they were still together. In another recent study,[4] married adults in a Western state were asked if they ever thought their marriage was in trouble. Nearly half (47%) said "yes," and nearly one in three (29%) said that at some time they had thought about divorce. About one in ten (11%) said they had talked to their spouse about a divorce in the last three years.

One such couple we know worked through a difficult situation with infidelity, one of the most difficult marital offenses to overcome. Four years after the affair they both said they had never been happier. The couple was happy that they had worked through the infidelity, which seemed impossible at the time of discovery. As a result of working things out, their four children were able to have continued and uninterrupted access to each other as well as live in a home with both parents. Both spouses had gone through forgiveness, healing, and changing. Although this couple's decision to work on why the affair occurred and the aftermath of the affair may not be right for every couple, they were happy about their decision to stay married and report being stronger for having successfully worked through a very tough situation. In similar cases of marital infidelity, a large majority of couples find that with proper help and support, they can move past the hurt and betrayal of the affair and develop a more intimate connection with each other.

Individuals at the crossroads of divorce can sometimes feel like they have to choose between two competing options: "Do I divorce so that I can find happiness again, or do I stay together for the family's sake and remain unhappy?" We think that this is a false choice. There is good evidence to suggest that with the proper help and willingness on the part of both spouses, many marriages that might otherwise end in divorce can become healthy, vibrant, and supportive. This chapter explains that if couples can stick it out through tough times, get decent support to look at their own contribution to the state of the marriage, and make thoughtful changes, their marriage is likely to become happy again. And there are helpful resources for those willing to work at it. The next chapter explores whether divorce is a reliable path to happiness for most adults.

A. Can unhappy marriages become happy again?

It may be difficult to face the issues that you and your spouse are struggling with, but research suggests that couples who courageously confront their problems, learn specific relationship skills, and stay together usually end up happy again down the road. Long-term unhappiness in marriage is uncommon. In a national study, only about 10% of individuals say at any particular time that they are unhappy in their marriages, and only about 2% say they are very unhappy.[5] As this study followed these couples over the next 5 years, they found that about 20% of these unhappy individuals did divorce. But about 80% hung on and were still married. The better news is that most of those who hung on weren't miserable. Half of unhappily married adults who avoided divorce ended up happily married to the same spouse 5 years later. And the unhappiest individuals improved the most; more than three quarters of the unhappiest individuals who avoided divorce said they were now happy. Another 20% of unhappily married adults reported improvement; they were no longer unhappy but not yet in the happy range. About 10% of unhappily married individuals were still married but still unhappy 5 years later. Couples can demonstrate incredible resilience. They seem to be able to overcome very serious problems in their marriages and often find happiness again. And fortunately, violence in these unhappy relationships was not very common; 23% of those that divorced and 15% of those that stayed together reported that an argument had gotten physical at least once.

Of course, we don't know your situation. Only you can decide what is best for you and your family. (And maybe this decision has been forced on you by your spouse.) We do hope, however, that you will give serious thought to the possibility of trying to strengthen your marriage rather than ending it. You may benefit from Exercise 2.1, "Hanging On or Moving On?" at the end of this chapter.

In our interview with Aaron, he told us how he and his wife hung on through bad times in their marriage. Reflecting on those times more than 20 years later, he was grateful they hung on.

> For a number of different reasons, we really struggled early on in our marriage. We were in love but we weren't prepared for things. We were more different from one another than we thought. I think people make too much about "compatibility," but yeah, I was amazed at how different we were. My expectations about what marriage was and how things would be were different from my experience of it all, you know, and I blamed her for that, I guess. I was kinda immature. And she brought some family baggage with her into the marriage that took a long time to work through. ... And a couple of times she spoke the "D-word" [divorce]. It devastated me. It hurt like nothing I've ever felt. I felt like a failure. But somehow we hung on. I grew up more and

became more realistic with my expectations. She was able to get some help and overcome some of her baggage from an abusive father. Over time, we just learned to love and accept each other more. And I guess having gone through hard times like that, you know, you just build an even stronger bond. I'm not saying we have a perfect marriage, but we have a strong, happy marriage ... and an intact family. We've built a wonderful life together and raised some wonderful children ... . It's scary to think about how close we came to maybe giving that up.

As we will discuss in Chapter 3, some divorced individuals express regret that they and their ex-spouse did not work harder to try to save their marriage. Divorce does not, by itself, make life better. One divorced man said this about his experience after divorce: "Divorce makes it so you lose all the good things that you had in your marriage and you get to keep all the fighting and contention." We'll discuss this further in the next chapter.

The rest of this chapter will discuss ways that individuals and couples can try to improve and strengthen their marriages, including seeking out marriage education classes, getting help from a marriage counselor, and self-guided efforts. Perhaps in your circumstances, however, strengthening your marriage isn't an option. Still, it may be valuable for you to be aware of the information in the next few sections to help you build a healthier relationship in the future.

B. Can couples improve their own marriages without outside help? How?

It may be surprising to learn that most couples who go from being unhappy to happy in their marriages do not get help from outside experts such as marriage therapists. Of course, some do seek help from a trained, professional counselor, and some seek help from a religious leader. Some seek informal help from trusted friends or family members. But some are able to overcome serious issues by themselves with effort and the passage of time. Sometimes the problem has to do more with circumstances outside the marriage that place stress on a relationship— for instance, a job loss or the death of a family member or a health problem—and eventually the stress goes away.[6] Others work on improving their relationship by themselves. Fran told us her story about this. Her first marriage ended early when she discovered her husband's infidelity. She remarried, but hit some hard times with some basic differences common among men and women. "Fran" described her feelings about the looming possibility of another divorce:

> For me, anxiety, fear, anger, failure again. Inadequate
> feelings. For him, anger, frustration, very similar feelings to
> mine, but only compounded with the male ego, which is a
> very strong source of energy. He was more emotional than I
> about it, because I had been thinking about it a long time,
> and he, being himself, said to me, "I didn't know anything
> was wrong." And then we talked. When I communicated
> how I felt, he, being the intelligent man he was, understood
> perfectly. ... We knew that the children were the future.
> They were our future ... . They were what we were actually
> about. We had more to gain from staying together than being
> apart. We both had to put our egos aside. ... We both had to
> look at ourselves. ... We started trying. We didn't just wait
> for things to happen. We scheduled things for ourselves. Not
> just routine, routine, routine. Every Saturday we had
> something to do for ourselves. We had a time for Deron and
> I, and we had a time for the family.

Fran and Deron worked through their hard times on their own with communication, understanding, and willingness to change. Years later as we interviewed Fran, she described a rich, rewarding, long-term marriage; she was sure she made the right decision to work through their problems.

Fran and Deron's story is one marked by putting forth specific effort to make the relationship a priority. They had to carve out time in their busy schedules to be together. They had to talk about topics that made them a bit uncomfortable. They made a commitment to put their egos aside and take an honest and open look at their own contributions to their relationship problems. It was not easy to do any of these things because they had become accustomed to "letting the relationship come to them" instead of them investing in the relationship with hopes that their investment of time and attention would pay off with a healthier relationship.

Drs. Wallace Goddard and James Marshall, marriage researchers and educators from the University of Arkansas, compare nurturing a marriage to growing a garden. If you're interested in eating the fruit of the garden, you've got to first plant, water, weed, cultivate, and watch over your garden so it can reach its potential.[7] And in some cases dealing with some manure may actually strengthen the harvest!

In Box 2.1, we provide a list of excellent books and websites dealing with marriage and how to improve your relationship that may help you.

C. Are there classes that can help couples have a healthy, happy marriage?

Marriages don't come with an instruction manual, but maybe it would help if they did. It seems like you have to go through some formal training for just about any license you get, except a marriage license—simply register, pay the fee, and you're ready to get married. In some states, like Texas, however, you can have all or part of the marriage license fee waived if you attend a certain number of hours of premarital relationship education.

Unlike marriage therapy, which is designed to help couples reclaim their marriage once things have gone wrong, relationship education is designed to boost the communication and conflict-resolution skills of couples who are currently married or are thinking about getting married. It is intended to help couples who have only a few or moderate problems to strengthen their relationship. However, new research suggests that couples with more distress and struggles in life may benefit more from what relationship education has to offer. This seems to be the case regardless of the couple's ethnicity or racial background.[8]

Research suggests that only about one in three individuals invest in any kind of formal relationship education or training before marrying, although that figure appears to be increasing for recently marrying couples, and almost all think that it is valuable.[9] Similarly, we suspect that a minority of married couples takes marriage enrichment classes to enhance their marriage and improve their communication skills. Probably most are unaware of the many resources available to help them form and sustain a healthy, happy marriage or to repair a struggling marriage. Some states have websites listing marriage and relationship education classes for the general public.[10]

Since the late 1990s, a growing number of states and communities have been investing in more resources to provide couples with marriage education classes.[11] This has happened on a large scale in states like Alabama, California, Oklahoma, Texas, and Utah and in communities like Chattanooga, Tennessee, and Washington, D.C.

Marriage education is also different from marriage counseling or therapy as it brings individuals and couples together, usually in groups of 10 to 20, and generally provides them with research-based information on what makes marriages work. Some classes are taught by highly trained professionals, but others are taught by individuals who just have a passion for strengthening marriages and have trained to teach a certain curriculum or program. Sometimes religious leaders or people they designate teach these classes. Both professionals and passionate lay people can be effective educators.[12]

Marriage education is offered in various places, such as churches, community settings, workplaces, hospitals, schools, and colleges. Some classes are targeted to specific groups of people, such as couples of a similar ethnic, racial, or religious identity, or couples who do not speak English. Many marriage education classes are offered for free, especially when they are run by religious organizations or supported by government funds. Other classes charge a fee or "tuition." Depending on the program, those fees can range from the cost of materials—about $20—to several hundred dollars. (While several hundred dollars seems like a lot of money, it is a lot less than the typical costs associated with marriage counseling or the cost of a divorce.) Most marriage education classes have about 12 hours of instruction and training, although some programs are a little shorter and a few are longer. Generally, couples are encouraged to attend marriage education classes together, but this may not be a requirement. The classes are interactive, but those who participate in the classes are not encouraged to share very private matters. Many who participate in marriage education classes say that it is helpful for them to hear others in the class talk about their challenges in marriage, but instructors usually control discussion so that people don't disclose highly personal and private issues that might make others uncomfortable.

Some who take marriage education classes are just trying to "tune-up" their relationships to prevent serious problems. Others are experiencing serious problems and have considered divorce. Many participants are in between, motivated to attend the class to help them because of some current concerns but not thinking seriously about divorce. In these classes, the focus is on learning skills, attitudes, behaviors, and principles that can strengthen and support an intimate and caring relationship. In most classes, there is a lot of emphasis on discovering the key ingredients for good communication and problem solving and practicing good communication skills. Some, but not all, classes take on specific topics like dealing with in-laws, managing money, or building a mutually satisfying sexual relationship. But again, the classes are different from marriage counseling that is typically done one-on-one or with a couple and one therapist; marriage education does not deal openly with an individual's or couple's private issues but addresses more globally the key ingredients to a healthy relationship.

Box 2.1 Self-Guided Resources Related to Marriage and Divorce

Books

❖ *The Divorce Remedy: The Proven 7-Step Program for Saving Your Marriage,* by Michele Weiner Davis. Simon & Schuster, 2001.

❖ *The Seven Principles for Making Marriage Work,* by John M. Gottman & Nan Silver. Three Rivers Press, 2000.

❖ *Can My Marriage Be Saved? True Stories of Saved Marriages,* by Mae Chambers & Erika Chambers. Pass It On Publications, 2008.

❖ *Fighting For Your Marriage,* by Howard Markman, Scott Stanley, & Susan Blumburg. Jossey-Bass, 2010.

❖ *The Power of Commitment: A Guide to Active, Lifelong Love,* by Dr. Scott M. Stanley. Jossey-Bass, 2005.

❖ *The Great Marriage Tune-Up Book: A Proven Program for Evaluating and Renewing Your Relationship,* by Dr. Jeffry H. Larson. Jossey-Bass, 2003.

❖ *Take Back Your Marriage,* by Dr. William J. Doherty. Guilford, 2001.

Websites

❖ www.prepare-enrich.com This website contains an online, self-guided relationship questionnaire for evaluating the strengths and weaknesses in your relationship, called "Couple Checkup." The program is done in your home with computer-generated feedback. It was developed by one of the world's leading relationship educators.

❖ www.couplecare.info This website introduces you to an inexpensive, self-guided program to work on improving your communication and other relationship skills. You do the work in your home; a trained facilitator will call you from time to time and ask if you have questions and discuss how things are going. The program was developed by a leading relationship expert.

❖ www.twoofus.org/marriage-advice/index.aspx This website, developed by the National Healthy Marriage Resource Center, has valuable resources for strengthening your marriage.

❖ www.divorcebusting.com This website has resources to connect you with a divorce-busting "coach."

Those who take a marriage and relationship education class almost always report that they enjoyed the class and felt that it helped their marriage. So what does the scientific research show? Can marriage education classes help couples—even struggling ones—improve their marriages? A lot of research has been done on this question. Many marriage education programs have been scientifically evaluated over the past 30 years. A study that reviewed all of the evaluation research on the effectiveness of marriage and relationship education concluded that it was helpful in strengthening communication and problem-solving skills and improving marital satisfaction for both men and women.[13] So there is pretty good evidence that marriage education can be helpful for couples. Also, research suggests that the effectiveness of marriage education doesn't wear off after just a couple of weeks; couples retain the skills they learned, at least for a while.[14] Of course, these are averages. Some couples may not benefit much from marriage education, but others benefit a great deal. Only a few studies have looked specifically at the effectiveness of marriage education for couples that are in serious distress and may be thinking about divorce, but these few studies suggest that distressed couples can benefit from marriage education.[15]

Overall, marriage education is able to help many couples build and maintain a healthier and happier marriage, even for those at the crossroads of divorce, like Jorge and Emily:

> Jorge saw the HARP [Hispanic Active Relationships Center, in Dallas, Texas] billboard as he was driving home one day. Since his relationship was about to end, the billboard caught his attention. He wrote down HARP's number and once he was home he told his wife about the billboard and that he wanted to call to get information. His wife, Emily, had given up on the relationship and was convinced that their marital problems did not have a solution. After Jorge called and received the workshop information, he convinced Emily to at least go and try it out. He asked her to give their relationship one last chance before signing their divorce papers.
>
> Emily was very angry, resentful, full of mixed emotions, and did not want to get hopes up too high. Both Emily and Jorge ended up staying for the whole 12-hour class. They are still together and are determined to make their marriage work. Thanks to the HARP workshops, they learned that it is okay to forgive each other and they discovered great tools to communicate better and resolve their issues. Emily and Jorge, standing in front of class with tears in their eyes,

spoke about how their lives and relationship had changed for good and how they will be forever thankful to HARP for having such a huge impact on their lives.[16]

Other attendees have reported that since attending the classes there was a greater feeling of peacefulness and calm in their home because the fighting had stopped. Still others have commented on how they have taught their own adult children some of the principles that they learned in marriage education classes and that their children have begun relating to one another in more healthy ways as a result.[17]

A successful marriage is about more than just making a good choice of whom to marry; it is also the result of applying specific skills. Brittany, a remarried mother with several children, expressed strong feelings about this when we interviewed her:

> In my first marriage we didn't have a great of line of communication, so now my thing is, are you willing to go to a seminar together and learn how to communicate better? How much are you willing to sacrifice and do to make it [your marriage] successful?

Box 2.2 describes several well-known and well-tested marriage education programs. If you're at all curious about how marriage or relationship education might help you or someone you know, you may benefit from Exercise 2.2 at the end of this chapter, "Thinking About Education to Strengthen Marriages."

D. Can marriage counseling help? How can I choose a good counselor?

For couples with serious relationship problems, marriage or relationship education classes may not be enough. For example, some come to marriage having had negative experiences in childhood or in previous relationships. In some cases, our early experiences of close relationships, such as watching our parents argue with or neglect each other (or avoid conflict all together), or having been in an abusive relationship, may have emotionally wounded us and made it difficult to trust a spouse. In these cases, couple therapy can help get the issues out in the open and work toward the resolution of deep-seated hurt and sadness. It can do this in a safe environment where our partner can be supportive and understanding of what we are going through now and how the past may be shaping our present marital relationship.

Box 2.2: Marriage and Relationship Education Programs

* *PREP* or *Prevention and Relationship Enhancement Program* (www.prepinc.com). This is one of the most tested programs, developed by researchers at the University of Denver, Drs. Howard Markman and Scott Stanley.

* *Art and Science of Love* (www.gottman.com/marriage). This program was developed by one of the premier marriage researchers in the world, Dr. John Gottman, at the University of Washington.

* *PREPARE/ENRICH* (www.prepare-enrich.com). This is one of the most widely used programs worldwide, developed by Dr. David Olson at the University of Minnesota. This program is based on years of research and includes a thorough relationship assessment prior to any recommendations being made for what skills are necessary to enhance the couple's relationship.

* *RE* or *Relationship Enhancement* (www.nire.org). This is one of the earliest programs, developed by Dr. Bernard Guerney, Jr., at Penn State University. It emphasizes listening with empathy.

* *Marriage Encounter* (www.wwme.org). This is a weekend marriage enrichment program. It is associated with the Roman Catholic Church but is open to all.

* *Retrouvaille* (www.retrouvaille.org). This is a weekend program dedicated to helping couples with very serious problems and possibly headed towards divorce to "rediscover" their relationship. (The French word for rediscovery is *retrouvaille*, pronounced "reh-troo-vi," with a long *i*.) It is associated with the Roman Catholic Church, but all couples are welcome.

* *Smart Steps* (www.stepfamilies.info/SmartSteps.php). This program is designed specifically for remarriages and stepfamilies. It focuses on building couple and family strengths while addressing the unique needs and issues that face stepfamilies. Children and adults attend together in separate sessions then come together at the end for shared activities. The program was designed by Dr. Francesca Adler-Baeder at Auburn University.

Individuals and couples who are thinking about divorce should seriously consider seeing a licensed marriage and family therapist. Dr. William J. Doherty, a noted marriage scholar and therapist from the

University of Minnesota, argues that individuals have a responsibility to themselves, their children, and their communities to try and save a marriage when there are serious problems. He argues that just as it is wrong for someone not to seek treatment for a life-threatening physical illness when there is a reasonable chance for a cure, it is wrong not to seek help to overcome relationship problems that threaten the marriage.[18] Studies show that 80% of couples see some improvement in their relationship after visiting a marriage counselor.[19] Forty to fifty percent say almost all of their major problems were resolved.[20] Unfortunately, other surveys suggest that only about half who divorce get marital counseling (either religious or secular).[21]

For Doug and Keisha, however, a couple who had serious marital problems early on in their marriage and talked at length about divorce, marriage counseling made a big difference:

> One of the things we've worked on since [we decided to try and save our marriage]; we've actually gone to a lot of counseling. ... Yeah, it's been really helpful. ... I think it (counseling) opened up a backbone of stability for us. We've done some things that we never thought we'd do.

A recent study of women who had been thinking about divorce but who ultimately decided to stay married discussed how therapy was helpful. The women in this study said that therapy provided a "space" for the couple to discuss their relationship.

> I would definitely say it (decision to not divorce) was influenced by therapy mostly because going to therapy creates space to have difficult conversations that I think couples in general do not have. Because they're afraid to have them.

Therapy also offered a place where the spouses were more accountable to each another and where they were encouraged to act differently toward one another (e.g., more understanding and sympathetic). In therapy these individuals felt totally understood by another person, which then helped the couple reconnect and gain security in their marriage.[22] Most of the people in this study reported valuing their therapist's neutrality; they felt as though the therapist wasn't pushing for a specific outcome, either to divorce or stay married. But a few really appreciated a therapist who was up front about wanting to help the couple create a healthier marriage and avoid divorce.

Importantly, this study reported factors outside of therapy that also made a difference in deciding to stay married. Concerns about the children, seeing one's spouse work hard on the relationship, discovering hidden loving feelings, and realizing the tough road of divorce also contributed to the decision to stay married.

> I feel like it would be more complicated to get divorced and then have me get remarried, him get remarried, and then we have a daughter together and then we have stepchildren. I feel like it complicates things beyond what we need to do to make our relationship work. And so that's been a real driving force for me and trying to stay positive and try to keep going to counseling and keep working through things.

One thing that people worry about is how to choose a good therapist; not all therapists are created equal when it comes to working on your marriage. Therapists who only work with individuals are more likely to see only one side of a marital problem. In these cases it is very difficult for the therapist to know if the version of reality that is being presented is 100% accurate. Without all sides of the marital story, it is extremely difficult to provide sound counsel or advice. In many cases therapists who work only with individuals use the standard of "personal happiness" to guide their counseling. This standard suggests "if you're not happy in your marriage, you should get out, because your happiness is the most important thing." While there's nothing wrong with the pursuit of happiness, research tells us that individual happiness waxes and wanes over the course of most marriages. So, using a standard of personal happiness at one moment in time to judge whether or not a marriage can be healthy and fulfilling may be a bit misleading.

We also know that many couples become unhappy in their marriages because they stop investing in their relationship when the demands of young children and demanding work seem more urgent. Indeed, the seeds of most divorces begin to grow slowly with people taking their marriage for granted and stopping the investment of time and energy into their relationship. Once this happens it is very easy to declare, with some confidence, that the marriage is not "making me happy" and "I should consider moving on." In reality, most of these marriages can be saved by merely turning more attention toward the relationship, healing past resentments, and discovering things about your partner that you never knew. Often times, having a competent therapist, can help facilitate this process.

Here are some tips on choosing a counselor or therapist and getting the most out of marriage therapy:

❖ *Find a therapist with specific education, experience, and a license to practice marriage and family therapy.* Therapists who advertise as couple therapists may only be trained in individual therapy, which differs dramatically from couple therapy. Ask potential therapists if they received formal education and supervised training in couple or marriage therapy. Also, ask what percentage of the therapist's work is with couples.[23] Those who specialize in and do a lot of couple therapy may have greater experience. In some states, there are formal associations of professional, licensed marriage and family therapists that maintain a list of licensed marriage and family therapists (LMFTs). (See www.therapistlocator.net to find a qualified provider in your area.)

❖ *Choose a counselor or therapist who is committed to helping you save your marriage.* An effective marital therapist focuses on the couple as a unit, rather than as individuals. Focusing only on individual needs may lead a therapist to advocate divorce before working hard to solve relationship problems. Ask potential therapists about their views of marriage and divorce. Ask what they would choose between saving a troubled marriage and suggesting a couple separate. Also, ask how many of the couples they see stay together.[24] Another good idea (based on your comfort level) is to ask friends or co-workers if they have had good experiences in marriage counseling, or if they could make a recommendation. In doing this you may find that a concerned friend will be an advocate for you and your relationship. An excellent resource for finding a good marriage therapist is the National Registry of Marriage Friendly Therapists (www.marriagefriendlytherapists.com). Therapists listed there have the highest training standards in the country and also commit to a set of principles for doing therapy that assures that they will work very hard to help you repair your marriage before exploring the possibility of divorce.

❖ *Make sure your counselor or therapist has a clear plan of action that is followed through.* Effective marital therapy requires structure and direction. If counseling sessions do not seem to be going anywhere, consider a new therapist.[25]

❖ *Understand that different types of counseling or therapy produce different results.* Most forms of therapy produce short-term benefits. However, to achieve long-term results, therapy should focus on changing emotions and thoughts, rather than just teaching communication and other skills. Successful therapy helps couples truly understand one another and offers a plan for facilitating a connection between marital partners. If a therapist seems to focus only on changing what you should do (e.g., go on more date nights, bring her flowers), without also emphasizing the need to hear how your partner feels so that you can change how you feel and think in the relationship, the positive benefits may not last.[26]

❖ *Do not assume that more expensive counseling or therapy is better.* Just because a therapist requires a higher fee does not mean you are getting better therapy.[27] Also, although therapy seems expensive, if it can save your marriage it will be less expensive in the long run than a divorce. Also, some therapists have sliding fees and will reduce the costs for lower income couples. Some people have accessed marital counseling services through their company's Employee Assistance Program (EAP). Contact the human resource representative at your workplace to see if your company offers EAP services. In addition, many universities have therapy training programs and offer counseling with therapists-in-training at low rates. (For a list of accredited Marriage and Family Therapy training programs located at a university in your area go to www.aamft.org) Also, some insurance companies will pay for a limited number of sessions with a therapist who can help you with your relationship. This is especially the case if your marital situation is causing you or your spouse emotional difficulties such as anxiety or depression. If you have insurance, check to see if your insurer will pay for this benefit. Some families receive assistance from Medicaid. Medicaid often helps pay for counseling for individuals, couples, and families.

❖ *Consider working with religious leaders or counselors.* Many people prefer to work with religious leaders or counselors because they are more confident that they will share similar values.[28] Several of the people we interviewed while we were writing this guidebook mentioned how guidance from their religious leader was important to them. Sometimes a religious leader acts as a full-fledged marriage counselor. However, not all religious leaders have the training and experience to effectively counsel married couples. So the considerations listed above should also be applied to religious counselors. In most cases, a religious leader will still be able to point you in the right direction even if she or he does not feel qualified to help you with your marriage. Some religious groups also provide programs to help couples at the crossroads of divorce. For example,

Retrouvaille (www.retrouvaille.org), sponsored by the Roman Catholic Church but available to all, is designed to help couples save their marriages from a faith-based perspective. The program is taught by couples that once had serious problems but successfully avoided divorce.

❖ *Stick with it.* The couples that show the most improvement in therapy are those that stick with it.[29] If the above guidelines are met, avoid dropping out early. Oftentimes it is easy to consider leaving therapy prematurely because the initial struggles you began working on will improve significantly—sometimes beyond your expectations. However, seasoned therapists will acknowledge that there is a big difference between early success in therapy that can eliminate some surface issues and longer term therapy that can get more at the heart of a couple's problems. Consider committing to a certain number of hour-long sessions, say eight to ten, and then evaluate how successful they have been before leaving therapy altogether or switching to a different therapist.

❖ *One-partner therapy can be effective.* While having both husband and wife together in therapy is usually ideal, if one partner cannot or will not attend, therapy can still be beneficial to the couple.[30] If only one partner will be attending therapy, it is even more important that the therapist is committed to your marriage and is experienced in couple therapy.

Discernment Counseling. Many couples at the crossroads of divorce would benefit from a new form of counseling called "discernment counseling" being pioneered at the University of Minnesota. Discernment counseling was designed to help people who are considering divorce but are not 100% sure if it is the right decision. It is a short-term counseling model (one to five sessions) that focuses more on seeing if a couple's problems can be solved rather than trying to solve them. Discernment counseling helps people decide if they should work on their marriage or continue toward divorce. Discernment counseling is designed specifically for couples on the brink of divorce, where the couple has a difficult time seeing eye-to-eye, and is an ideal way of engaging couples to see if there is any possible way to restore health to their relationship. The overall goal of discernment counseling is to help people arrive at a place of clarity and confidence in determining the future of their relationship, whatever that may be. Our experience is that most people who are thinking about divorce have a lot on their mind and can get overwhelmed with all the things they are thinking about. A place to go to get clarity and confidence is a valuable resource. For more information about discernment counseling or the Minnesota Couples on the Brink Project and a list of therapists (some in your area) who have trained in this model visit: www.mncouplesonthebrink.org

You may benefit from Exercise 2.3, "Thinking About Marriage Counseling," at the end of this chapter.

E. Do divorcing couples sometimes reconcile and get back together? When is reconciliation likely to be successful?

As we pointed out earlier in this chapter, many marriages go from happy to unhappy and back to happy over the course of a life time. Reconciliation is a process of getting back together that requires the full participation of both spouses. Researchers estimate that 10% of married couples in the United States have experienced a separation and reconciliation.[31] Researchers also estimate that about one in three couples who separate later try to reconcile, but only about one third of those who try actually succeed.[32] One study estimated that about one third of couples who attempt to reconcile were still married a year later.[33]

One couple we know that had several children reconciled after realizing that the grass was not greener on the other side of the divorce fence. After the divorce, one of the spouses was considering remarrying another person. Through her dating the other man, she realized that no relationship is perfect and that although this new partner did not have some of the characteristics of her ex-husband that really bugged her, there were other problems and complications with the new guy that did not exist in her original marriage. She decided to talk with her first husband before remarrying. Instead of the wife marrying someone else, the couple was able to reconcile and remarry. Their children were elated after enduring the every-other-weekend visiting schedule. The parents have now been happily remarried for many years.

In our interviews with various individuals who had been at the crossroads of divorce, we noticed that many tried to reconcile. But it's not easy, and success was elusive. Laura's story illustrates both the hope and the ultimate discouragement that can accompany reconciliation attempts:

> [My husband] came back about a month [after the separation] with all of his stuff at the front door. When I opened the front door, he told me, "I am coming home." And I'm like, "What?" And we had kind of talked through things. The thing was that we were really, really good friends. ... [Later] I discovered that I was 5 months pregnant! I was in

such shock I didn't know whether to be happy or sad. We (my mom and I) went up to see my husband and I couldn't even talk; I was in such shock. My mom told him that he was going to be a father and he was ecstatic. He truly, truly was, because he had wanted a child and he wanted me to be the mother of his child. ... I got really, really sick. Within a couple of days, I was in the hospital; I was bleeding already. ... Long story short, I couldn't get a hold of my husband [that night]. I was in the hospital the whole night and so I finally called his friend, and I said, "I know you don't want to hear me, but I can't find my husband and I just lost the baby, so if you could please just call him." My husband was at my mother's front door within probably about 10 minutes. I saw the stamp on his hand. He had been at a nightclub all night, and that just put it all in perspective for me. I said, "Mom, I don't care what it takes, but we need to push this divorce through."

There are a number of factors that make reconciliation more likely, many of which were not going in Laura's favor. Couples who have the same religion and attend religious services regularly are more likely to reconcile. So are those who were older when they got married, who are closer in age, and who have more education.[34] One researcher who interviewed couples who had faced difficult marital problems but had successfully reconciled discovered two interesting points that contributed to their success.[35] First, these couples made reconciliation their top priority. Commitment was essential and was demonstrated by their actions: accepting responsibility for their mistakes, changing behavior, and offering forgiveness. Second, they did not do it alone; they sought out religious and professional help and received the support of family and friends. Many of the couples had little hope of fixing things when they began but were able to persevere. They attended marriage education classes, seminars, or retreats, read marriage books, or went to counseling. Some made significant changes in their environment, such as moving or changing churches. They drew on the personal history they had built together that included their children, all they had invested in the relationship, and their years of friendship. They acknowledged the strengths in their relationship and cut out anything that would not aid in reconciliation.

Another couple we know who divorced realized too late that their hostile attitudes toward each other in a time of crisis led to their divorce. The problem escalated as family, friends, and co-workers got involved in the marital conflict. Neither spouse made a sincere attempt to communicate and because the divorce was filed in haste to show the seriousness of the problem, neither was willing to try and make the relationship work. A year later, as they sat down and discussed the issues that led to the divorce, they decided to make reconciliation their top priority. The couple regretted their hasty decision and lack of problem-solving skills at the time of their divorce. They remarried and have since had children and have been happily married for more than a decade.

In addition, researchers have found that insecure individuals are more likely to try to keep an unhappy marriage together, probably because they are afraid of not being in a relationship or afraid they will not find another relationship. Insecurity is grounded in feelings of low self-worth and fear of abandonment. Insecure individuals are more likely over time to feel unhappy in their marriages, but also more likely to be motivated to try to keep their marriages together, despite their dissatisfaction.[36] Related to feelings of insecurity are feelings of extreme dependence. A mutual dependence between spouses is important to a healthy marriage, but extreme dependence is a sign of insecurity; these individuals depend almost completely on their spouses to fulfill their feelings of self-worth and security. As a result, these individuals are more likely to try to keep their marriages together, even if they are in unhealthy relationships.[37] Good therapists can assist people with feelings of insecurity and extreme dependence,[38] helping perhaps to turn an unhappy marriage into a happy marriage and avoiding the further negative effects of divorce on insecure adults and other family members.[39]

We recognize that reconciliation may not be wise in many cases, especially when there has been abuse in the family. (We discuss abuse and infidelity in Chapter 4.) The reality is that many who try to get back together to make things work do not succeed. But some do succeed with dedication and effort. You may benefit from exercise 2.4, "Thinking About Reconciliation," at the end of the chapter.

F. What if I'm willing to try to save my marriage but my spouse doesn't seem willing?

It is hard to imagine anything more frustrating than wanting to save your marriage when your spouse isn't interested. One national study found that in four out of five divorces, one spouse did not want the divorce.[40] Many spouses in this situation feel powerless; they don't believe that they "deserve" divorce. But in our legal system one spouse can make that decision alone regardless of the circumstances. Legally, you don't have a lot of options. Only half of states these days have mandatory waiting periods before granting a divorce; the typical waiting period for states that have them is only 30 days. A few states have "time out" laws that allow you to go to a judge and ask that the legal divorce process be suspended for a brief period to pursue marriage counseling.[41] You can ask your divorce lawyer about this option, although many lawyers don't even know about these options.

You may feel that you would do anything to make things right. This desire can be a real turning point for some marriages. If you are willing to do whatever it would take to make your marriage work, think seriously about what your spouse is asking from you now—more space, more partnership with money or housework, more interaction with your children, less nagging, less time with buddies, less time on the computer or the TV. What might happen if you honored your spouse's request? If your spouse were able to see you differently than he or she has before, what might be the result? One book that may be helpful if you are in this situation is *The Divorce Remedy: The Proven 7-Step Program for Saving Your Marriage,* by Michele Weiner-Davis.

Some spouses are willing to give things a second chance once they see that their partners are truly committed and sincere about change. Other spouses feel like there is just "too much water under the bridge." Your marriage may or may not be possible to save at this point; your spouse may not reconsider, no matter how much you try to make things better.

Although it may be hard to imagine your future at all, and although it may seem too early even to consider it, most people do remarry. Understanding now what you can do to be a better spouse can help you in a future marriage. So, you may want to consider: How did this marriage get to this point? What are some of the things that you could have done differently to make the marriage better a year ago, or 2 years ago, or 10 years ago?

G. What is a "healthy" marriage?

In all this discussion about ways to repair marriages and keep families together, some may not have a clear idea of what a healthy marriage even looks like. Perhaps some grew up in a home and neighborhood without seeing good examples of a healthy marriage. So we want to clarify what it means to have a healthy marriage. While there are many opinions about this, we think one of the best definitions comes from a research organization called Child Trends that examined hundreds of studies to come up with 10 characteristics that define a healthy marriage.[42]

❖ *Commitment:* Spouses have a long-term perspective toward their relationship; they intend to persevere when troubles come up; they are willing to sacrifice their personal needs for each other. Commitment involves dedication and constraints. We talk more about commitment in Chapter 4.

❖ *Satisfaction:* Overall, individuals are happy and satisfied with their relationship. This does not mean that marriage is without problems and challenges, or that married couples don't go through periods when they are not happy in their marriages. But overall, healthy marriages are happy and satisfying relationships. About 90% of married people at any one time say they are very satisfied with their marriage.[43]

❖ *Communication:* Couples interact with each other to exchange information and solve problems in respectful, positive ways. The way that couples communicate with each other—in positive and negative ways—is one of the strongest indicators of how healthy a relationship is and whether the marriage will last.[44]

❖ *Effective Conflict Resolution:* Virtually all couples have differences and disagreements; some can be very serious. How they handle these disagreements can make the difference between a healthy and unhealthy relationship. An important indicator of a healthy marriage is a couple's ability to deal with stress and conflict without criticism, contempt, or defensiveness.[45]

❖ *Lack of Violence and Abuse:* While differences and disagreements are a normal part of marriage, aggression and violence indicate an unhealthy relationship. This includes verbal, physical, emotional, and sexual aggression and abuse. Abuse of any children in the relationship also is unacceptable.

❖ *Fidelity or Faithfulness:* Spouses are sexually faithful to each other; they keep intimate physical relationships within the bonds of marriage. Virtually all married individuals endorse this value. Infidelity is one of the most common reasons people give for a divorce; about half of divorced individuals say it was a contributing factor in their divorce.[46] And individuals can be emotionally unfaithful to their spouse without actual sexual involvement.[47] Most married individuals remain sexually faithful to their spouses; research suggests that only about 10%–15% of women and 25% of men report they were unfaithful to their spouse while they were married.[48]

❖ *Intimacy and Emotional Support:* Couples in a healthy marriage are physically and emotionally intimate with each other. They trust, care for, and love each other.

❖ *Friendship and Spending Time Together:* While couples are different in the amount of time they spend interacting and doing things together, in a healthy marriage couples enjoy being together. They are friends; they respect each other and enjoy each other's company. Friendship and time together may be more important to some cultural groups than to others,[49] but especially in America, they are highly valued in a marriage.

❖ *Commitment to Children:* Not all married couples have children or have children living with them. But in a healthy marriage with children, the couple is committed to the development and well-being of all their children.

❖ *Duration and Legal Status:* The optimal environment for raising children is a family with two biological (or adoptive) parents in a stable, healthy marriage. Believing in the permanence of the relationship actually helps to sustain a healthy marriage; those who don't believe that marriage should be permanent have a harder time sustaining a healthy marriage.[50] Marriage represents an important legal status. Marriage is not only a commitment to another person but also a public commitment to society to behave in certain constructive ways. In turn, society supports the relationship and the children in that union.[51]

It's important to remember that couples have healthy marriages to varying degrees; it's not an either/or situation. All marriages have ups and downs. But these characteristics are a good definition of a healthy marriage. You may want to evaluate the strengths and weaknesses of your marriage with Exercise 2.5, "Elements of a Healthy Marriage: How Important Are They?" at the end of the chapter.

2.1: Hanging On or Moving On?

As was mentioned in Chapter 2, most individuals who say they are unhappy in their marriage, but have decided to hang on for a few years, end up saying that they are happy again. This exercise is designed to help you think about hanging on as a possible option for you. Of course, we realize that some people don't have a choice; their spouse is insisting on a divorce.

A. What are some reasons for hanging on and trying to make things work out? List them here:

_____

_____

_____

_____

_____

_____

B. Are there some reasons why it might not be wise to hang on and try to make things work out? List them here:

_____

_____

_____

_____

_____

_____

C. What are the stresses on or within your marriage that are making things difficult? Consider both inside stresses (e.g., kids demand a lot of time) and outside stresses (e.g., demanding job, financial pressures)? Then think about whether those stresses are likely to change in a positive way over the next few years? Are there things you could do to reduce those stresses?

What is the stress?	How likely is it to change?	What could you do to reduce the stress?

What have you learned from thinking about these issues? What do you think will happen if you hang on for the next few years and try and make things work? Write down your thoughts here:

_____

_____

_____

_____

_____

2.2: Thinking About Education to Strengthen Marriages

What have you done recently to try and strengthen your marriage? Some couples, even those with some serious problems who are thinking about divorce, try some educational resources to try and improve their relationship.

A. What books have you read to try and strengthen your marriage? How helpful were they? If you haven't done this, look at the list of suggested books in Box 2.1 in this chapter and pick one to read, either by yourself or together as a couple. Write down the title here and a set a goal for a date to read the book.

_____

_____

_____

B. What websites have you visited to try and strengthen your marriage? How helpful were they? If you haven't done this, look at the list of suggested websites in Box 2.1 in this guidebook and pick one to browse, either by yourself or together as a couple. Write down the name and address of the website and set a goal for a date to visit the site or do it right now.

_____

_____

_____

C. Have you ever taken a marriage-strengthening class together (including a marriage preparation education class)? If so, what do you remember about that experience? What did you learn? How did you feel about the experience? Do you think it was helpful? Write down your thoughts here:

_____

_____

_____

_____

_____

_____

D. Do you think you would benefit from taking a marriage-strengthening class, either by yourself or with your spouse, to help you resolve problems, communicate more effectively, and increase your satisfaction with your marriage? Why or why not? As you answer this question, consider whether you would feel comfortable or awkward in class with other couples working on improving their marriages. Write down your thoughts here:

_____

_____

_____

_____

_____

E. Are you aware of some marriage-strengthening classes in your area? Does your church or other religious group offer marriage-strengthening classes? Box 2.2 lists a number of popular programs and their websites. Do a little investigation of local resources and write down a few possibilities that you might be interested in here:

_____

_____

_____

_____

_____

2.3: Thinking About Marriage Counseling

People have different thoughts and feelings about seeking marriage counseling, some positive, some negative, and some just unsure. Interestingly, most couples do not get counseling before they divorce. This exercise is designed to help you sort out your own thoughts and feelings about getting some formal marriage counseling to help you with the challenges you are experiencing in your marriage.

A. Have you had some marriage counseling before? __ No __ Yes. If yes, how was that experience for you? Was it helpful? Did you give an honest effort or could you have done better? Why did you stop going?

_____

_____

_____

_____

B. How comfortable do you think you would feel getting marriage counseling? Write down some of your thoughts and feelings about the following questions. Also, think about how your spouse might answer these questions.

❖ Are you willing to take an honest look at yourself and your part in how your relationship is struggling and how it could be improved?

Your feelings:

_____

_____

_____

_____

Your spouse's feelings:

_____

_____

_____

_____

❖ Are you willing to allow a marriage counselor help you learn to communicate more effectively with your spouse?

Your feelings:

_____

_____

_____

_____

Your spouse's feelings:

_____

_____

_____

_____

❖ How willing are you to share deep, personal thoughts and feelings in a counseling session?

Your willingness to discuss feelings:

_____

_____

_____

_____

Your spouse's willingness to discuss feelings:

_____

_____

_____

_____

❖ How willing are you to do "homework" assignments to work on your relationship outside of marriage counseling, if your counselor asks you to?

Your willingness:

_____

_____

_____

_____

Your spouse's willingness:

_____

_____

_____

_____

❖ Overall, how comfortable do you think you would be with marriage counseling?

Your feelings on the subject:

_____

_____

_____

_____

Your spouse's feelings on the subject:

_____

_____

_____

_____

C. If you belong to a religious organization, do you know if it offers some type of marriage counseling? __ No __ Yes. If yes, do you think you would feel more or less comfortable with counseling from a religious leader?
__ More comfortable __ Less comfortable. Why? _____

_____

_____

_____

_____

D. In this chapter we suggested various ways that you could find a good marriage counselor. Review these suggestions. Then, if you were to decide to get some counseling, write down how you would go about finding a good marriage counselor.

_____

_____

E. If you decide to get marriage counseling, how would you pay for it? Although some religious organizations offer free counseling, secular counselors charge a fee. Does your insurance company pay for marriage counseling? __ Yes __ No __ Unsure.

If your insurance company will pay for marriage counseling, how many sessions will they help pay for? ___ sessions. (You may need to consult with your insurance company or employer's human resources department to find this out.) If you would need to pay for marriage counseling yourself, how much would you be willing to pay? $ _____. (In Chapters 7 and 8 you will read more about how expensive a divorce can be; effective counseling is less costly.)

F. So overall, how willing do you think you and your spouse would be to get some marriage counseling? (Check the box that fits best.)

	Not at all Willing	A Little Willing	Somewhat Willing	Very Willing
You				
Your Spouse				

2.4. Thinking About Reconciliation

It's not uncommon for couples who are separated or heading for divorce to try and reconcile and keep trying to work things out. Sometimes reconciliation is successful but other times it is not. This brief exercise is designed to help you think about the possibility of reconciliation and how helpful it might be.

A. *Priorities.* Reconciliation is more likely to be successful when both spouses make strengthening the marriage a high priority. How committed would you be? How committed do you think your spouse would be? (Check the box that fits best.)

	Not at all Committed	A Little Committed	Somewhat Committed	Very Committed
You				
Your Spouse				

If you decided to reconcile, what specific things could you do to make strengthening your marriage a high priority? Think about big things, like going together to a marriage education class or marriage counseling. Also think about some small things, like a regular time each day to talk and reconnect, verbally greeting each other when arriving home, kissing when leaving the house, praying together daily, a weekly date, dropping some demands on your time, developing some shared interests, etc. Brainstorm some ideas and write them down:

_____

_____

_____

_____

Now think about these ideas. List two or three of the ideas that you think will be most effective below and make a plan for how you will do this:

Ways to prioritize my marriage:	How will I do it?
1.	1.
2.	2.
3.	3.
4.	4.

B. *Support.* Having the support of family members and friends for reconciliation helps. List important family members and friends and evaluate how supportive they would be.

List Family Member/ Friend	How supportive would this person be of reconciliation?			
	Not at all Supportive	Somewhat Supportive	Very Supportive	Why?

So overall, how much support would you have for reconciliation? Write down your thoughts here:

_____

_____

_____

_____

C. *Remembering the Good Times.* When you think back on your relationship, both before you got married and after, can you think of good, positive times? When couples are going through hard times, it is common to focus on the bad and not remember the good times and good features of the relationship. But if you can recall those good times and good aspects of the relationship, then you have a better chance of being able to work through your challenges and keep your marriage together. A marriage that was built on friendship and fondness sometimes can be revived, despite the challenges you are facing now. This exercise is designed to help you try to remember the good times and good parts of your relationship.

❖ What do you remember about dating your spouse? What attracted her or him to you? What did you enjoy doing together? Write down some of your thoughts here:

_____

_____

_____

_____

_____

❖ Why did you choose to marry your spouse? What influenced you to make the big decision to decide to spend your life together with this person? Write down your thoughts here:

_____

_____

_____

_____

_____

❖ Despite your current problems, what positive things do you still see in your marriage? What good characteristics do you still see in your spouse? Write down your thoughts here:

_____

_____

_____

_____

_____

❖ Have you gone through some tough times together before? What kept you going through those times? Write down your thoughts here:

_____

_____

_____

_____

_____

❖ If you have been able to remember some of the good features of your marriage and your spouse, it helps you to see the possibility of a better future. What have you learned by trying to remember the good times? Write down your thoughts here:

_____

_____

_____

_____

_____

_____

2.5: Elements of a Healthy Marriage: How Important Are They?

A. *Elements of a Healthy Marriage.* Researchers have identified 10 essential elements of a healthy marriage. How important are these 10 elements to you? For each of the 10 elements, make a quick judgment about how important it is to you.

Essential Element Definition	How important is this to you?		
	Not Important	Somewhat Important	Very Important
1. *Commitment:* Each spouse has a long-term perspective of the marriage and an intention to persevere through hard times; each spouse is committed to the well-being of the other.	0	1	3
2. *Satisfaction:* The marriage is a source of happiness for each spouse.	0	1	3
3. *Communication:* The couple is able to talk and communicate with each other in positive and respectful ways.	0	1	3
4. *Conflict Resolution:* The couple is able to handle differences and conflicts and solve problems in a positive way.	0	1	3
5. *Lack of Violence:* Neither spouse is abusive of other or their children, physically, psychologically, or sexually.	0	1	3
6. *Fidelity:* Spouses are sexually faithful to one another; sex is reserved for one's spouse and no one else.	0	1	3
7. *Friendship/Time Together:* Spouses are friends; they like and respect each other; they know each other well; they enjoy spending time together.	0	1	3
8. *Intimacy/Emotional Support:* Spouses trust, care, and love each other; they are affectionate.	0	1	3
9. *Commitment to Children:* Each spouse is committed to the well-being of all of their children.	0	1	3
10. *Duration/Legal Status:* A couple makes a formal legal commitment (marriage) and plans for the marriage to endure.	0	1	3

This was a very quick assessment of how important each of these elements of a healthy marriage is to you. People will differ in how important certain elements are. What have you learned by considering how important these elements are to you?

_____

_____

_____

Next is a little more detailed questionnaire to help you evaluate the different strengths and weaknesses in your relationship.

B. *Evaluating the Strengths and Weaknesses of Your Relationship.* If you are like most couples, your relationship has both weaknesses and strengths. How do you rate your relationship? What can you do to keep the strong areas strong? What can you do to improve the problem areas? This quiz can help you think about these questions.

The questions come from a research study that looked at the quality of relationships.[52] The study included 1,550 couples that are typical of all couples in the United States. The researchers who did this study found that a person's answers to the quiz can tell a lot about the quality of a relationship, but it's not perfect.

Here's how the quiz works: Answer these 30 questions and then add up the score. Then you can go through an exercise to find the strengths in your relationship and areas where you need to make improvements.

You can do the quiz on your own. If you feel comfortable, both you and your spouse could take the quiz separately, then share your results. Use the tips at the end to help you appreciate your strengths and talk about ways to work on your weaknesses.

For each question, circle the number below the answer that best matches your feelings. Remember, the usefulness of this quiz depends on how much you know about yourself and your partner and how honest you are in your responses.

In your relationship, how satisfied are you with:					
	Very Dissatis-fied	Dissatis-fied	Neutral	Satis-fied	Very Satis-fied
1. Your overall relationship with your spouse?	1	2	3	4	5
2. The quality of your communication?	1	2	3	4	5
3. The love you experience?	1	2	3	4	5
How is your SPOUSE in your relationship?					
	Never	Rarely	Some-times	Often	Very Often
4. My spouse understands my feelings.	1	2	3	4	5
5. My spouse listens to me in an understanding way.	1	2	3	4	5
6. My spouse uses a tactless choice of words when she or he complains.	5	4	3	2	1
7. My spouse doesn't censor his/her complaints at all. She/he really lets me have it full force.	5	4	3	2	1
How often do these words or phrases describe YOU?					
8. Worrier	5	4	3	2	1
9. Nervous	5	4	3	2	1
	Never	Rarely	Some-times	Often	Very Often
9. Nervous	5	4	3	2	1
10. Depressed	5	4	3	2	1
11. Feel hopeless	5	4	3	2	1
12. Fight with others/lose temper	5	4	3	2	1
13. Easily irritated or mad	5	4	3	2	1
How often do these words/expressions describe YOUR SPOUSE?					
14. Worrier	5	4	3	2	1
15. Nervous	5	4	3	2	1
16. Depressed	5	4	3	2	1
17. Feel hopeless	5	4	3	2	1
18. Fight with others/lose	5	4	3	2	1

temper					
19. Easily irritated or mad	5	4	3	2	1

How much do you agree with the following statements about the family you grew up with?

	Strongly Disagree	Disagree	It Depends	Agree	Strongly Agree
20. I'm still having trouble dealing with some issues from my family while growing up.	5	4	3	2	1
21. Some issues from my family while growing up make it hard for me to form close relationships.	5	4	3	2	1

How often have the following areas been a problem in your relationship?

	Never	Rarely	Sometimes	Often	Very Often
22. Financial matters	5	4	3	2	1
23. Communication	5	4	3	2	1
24. Intimacy/sexuality	5	4	3	2	1
25. Parents/In-laws	5	4	3	2	1
26. Roles (who does what)	5	4	3	2	1
27. Time spent together	5	4	3	2	1
28. How often have you thought your relationship might be in trouble?	5	4	3	2	1
29. How often is your current SPOUSE violent toward you?	5	4	3	2	1
30. How often are YOU violent toward your current partner?	5	4	3	2	1

Score your quiz now. To score your quiz, just add up the numbers you circled. Your score should be between 30 and 150.

Your Score: _____

What Your Score Means: A higher number indicates more areas of strength and fewer areas of weakness. A lower number indicates more areas of weakness that you may need to work on to improve the quality of your relationship.

C. *Learn from the Quiz: What Are Your Strengths and Weaknesses?* All couples have strengths and challenges in their relationships. List and talk about your strengths and areas for improvement.

Strengths. For questions 1–5 in the *Strengths and Weaknesses of Your Relationship* quiz, a response of 4 or 5 says that these are strengths in your relationship. For questions 6–30 in the quiz, a response of 1 or 2 says that these are strengths in your relationship. So, from your answers to the quiz, list the greatest strengths in your relationship.

1. _____

2. _____

Think and talk about these strengths. Don't take them for granted. How can you maintain and nurture these strengths?

1. _____

_____

2. _____

_____

Weaknesses. For questions 1–5 in the *Strengths and Weaknesses of Your Relationship* quiz, a response of 1 or 2 says that these are challenges in your relationship. For questions 6–30 in the quiz, a response of 4 or 5 says that these are challenges in your relationship. From your answers to the quiz, list some challenges in your relationship that you could work on.

1. _____

_____

2. _____

_____

Think and talk together about these challenges. What can you do to improve in these areas?

1. _____

_____

2. _____

_____

There are easy ways to get a more detailed, in-depth look at all the different aspects of your relationship. For instance, here are some relationship inventories, or questionnaires, that you can access over the Internet that allow you to answer many detailed questions about your relationship with your spouse (privately). Then you get detailed feedback on the strengths and weaknesses in your relationship.

Relationship Inventory	Web Address	Associated University
FOCCUS	www.foccusinc.com	Creighton University
PREPARE/ ENRICH	www.prepare-enrich.com	University of Minnesota
RELATE	relate-institute.org	Brigham Young University

Endnotes to Chapter 2

[1] Viorst is an American author and journalist. Retrieved from http://www.lifesip.com/marriage-quotes.html

[2] Yeats was a noted Irish poet and literary figure who won a Nobel Prize for Literature. Retrieved from www.weird-websites.com/Quotes/Marriage-Wedding-Quotations-1.htm

[3] *With this ring ... A national survey on marriage in America.* Gaithersburg, MD: National Fatherhood Initiative (see p. 34).

[4] Schramm, D. G., Marshall, J. P., Harris, V. W., & George, A. (2003). *Marriage in Utah: 2003 baseline statewide survey on marriage and divorce.* Salt Lake City: Utah Department of Workforce Services (see pp. 15, 19–20).

[5] Waite, L., Browning, D., Doherty, W., Gallagher, M., Luo, Y., & Stanley, S. (2002). *Does divorce make people happy? Findings from a study of unhappy marriages.* New York: Institute for American Values (see p. 6).

[6] Waite, L., Browning, D., Doherty, W., Gallagher, M., Luo, Y., & Stanley, S. (2002). *Does divorce make people happy? Findings from a study of unhappy marriages.* New York: Institute for American Values (see pp. 15–29).

[7] Goddard, W. H. (2010). *The marriage garden: Cultivating your relationship so it grows and flourishes.* San Francisco: Jossey-Bass.

[8] Hawkins, A. J. (2013). *The forever initiative: A feasible public policy agenda to help couples form and sustain healthy marriages and relationships.* North Charleston, SC: CreateSpace Independent Publishing Platform.

[9] Stanley, S. M., Amato, P. R., Johnson, C. A., & Markman, H. J. (2006). Premarital education, marital quality, and marital stability: Findings from a large, random household survey. *Journal of Family Psychology, 20,* 117–126. Some other surveys in particular states have found slightly higher rates for couples marrying within the last decade. See Johnson, C. A., Stanley, S. M., Glenn, N. D., Amato, P. R., Nock, S. L., Markman, H. J., & Dion, M. R. (2002). *Marriage in Oklahoma: 2001 baseline statewide survey on marriage and divorce.* Stillwater, OK: Oklahoma State University Bureau for Social Research; Schramm, D. G., Marshall, J. P., Harris, V. W., & George, A. (2003). *Marriage in Utah: 2003 baseline statewide survey on marriage and divorce.* Salt Lake City: Utah Department of Workforce Services; *With this ring ... A national survey on marriage in America.* Gaithersburg, MD: National Fatherhood Initiative.

[9] Schramm, D. G., Marshall, J. P., Harris, V. W., & George, A. (2003). *Marriage in Utah: 2003 baseline statewide survey on marriage and divorce.* Salt Lake City: Utah Department of Workforce Services (see p. 21); *With this ring ... A national survey on marriage in America.* Gaithersburg, MD: National Fatherhood Initiative.

[10] For instance, in Oklahoma, see: www.okmarriage.org; in Utah, see: strongermarriage.org for a listing of classes.

[11] Hawkins, A. J. (2013). *The forever initiative: A feasible public policy agenda to help couples form and sustain healthy marriages and relationships.* North Charleston, SC: CreateSpace Independent Publishing Platform.

[12] Stanley, S. M., Markman, H. J., Prado, L. M., Olmos Gallo, P. A., Tonelli, L., St. Peters, M., Leber, B. D., Bobulinski, M., Cordova, A., & Whitton, S. (2001). Community based premarital prevention: Clergy and lay leaders on the front lines. *Family Relations, 50,* 67–76.

[13] Hawkins, A. J., Blanchard, V. L., Baldwin, S. A., & Fawcett, E. B. (2008). Does marriage and relationship education work? A meta-analytic study. *Journal of Consulting and Clinical Psychology, 76,* 723–734.

[14] Blanchard, V. L., Hawkins, A. J., Baldwin, S. A., & Fawcett, E. B. (2009). Investigating the effects of marriage and relationship education on couples' communication skills: A meta-analytic study. *Journal of Family Psychology, 23,* 203–214.

[15] Blanchard, V. L., Hawkins, A. J., Baldwin, S. A., & Fawcett, E. B. (2009). Investigating the effects of marriage and relationship education on couples' communication skills: A meta-analytic study. *Journal of Family Psychology, 23,* 203–214; Cordova, J. V., Scott, R. L., Dorian, M., Mirgain, S., Yaeger, D., & Groot, A. (2005). The Marriage Checkup: An indicated prevention intervention for treatment-avoidant couples at risk for marital deterioration. *Behavior Therapy, 36,* 301–309; Cowan, P. A., Cowan, C. P., Pruett, M., & Pruett, K. (in press). Supporting father involvement in low-income families: Interventions for fathers and couples. *Journal of Marriage and Family*; Cummings, E. M., Faircloth, W. B., Mitchell, P. M., Cummings, J. S., & Schermerhorn, A. C. (2008). Evaluating a brief prevention program for improving marital conflict in community families. *Journal of Family Psychology, 22,* 193–202.

[16] U.S. Department of Health & Human Services. (2009). *Emerging findings from the Office of Family Assistance Healthy Marriage and Responsible Fatherhood grant programs: A review of select grantee profiles and promising results.* (See p. 10).

[17] Daire, A. P., Harris, S. M., Carlson, R. G., Munyon, M. D., Rappleyea, D. L., Beverly, M. G., & Hiett, J. (2012). Fruits of improved communication: The experience of Hispanic couples in a relationship education program. *Journal of Couple and Relationship Therapy, 11,* 112–129.

[18] Doherty, W. J. (1992, May/June). Private lives, public values. *Psychology Today, 25,* 32–37, 82.

[19] Ward, D., & McCollum, E. (2005). Treatment effectiveness and its correlates in a marriage and family therapy training clinic. *American Journal of Family Therapy, 33*(3), 207–223.

[20] Bray, J., & Jouriles, E. (1995). Treatment of marital conflict and prevention of divorce. *Journal of Marital and Family Therapy, 21,* 461–473; Ward, D., & McCollum, E. (2005). Treatment effectiveness and its correlates in a marriage and family therapy training clinic. *American Journal of Family Therapy, 33*(3), 207–223.

[21] For instance, see: Schramm, D. G., Marshall, J. P., Harris, V. W., & George, A. (2003). *Marriage in Utah: 2003 baseline statewide survey on marriage and divorce.* Salt Lake City: Utah Department of Workforce Services (see p. 22).

[22] Kanewischer, E. J. W. (2012). *Deciding not to un-do the "I do": A qualitative study of the therapy experiences of women who consider divorce but decide to remain married.* Unpublished doctoral dissertation, University of Minnesota.

[23] Doherty, W. J. (1999). *How therapy can be hazardous to your marital health.* Retrieved from http://www.smartmarriages.com/hazardous.html

[24] Doherty, W. J. (1999). *How therapy can be hazardous to your marital health.* Retrieved from http://www.smartmarriages.com/hazardous.html; Doherty, W. J. (1995). *Soul searching: Why psychotherapy must promote moral responsibility.* New York: BasicBooks; Weiner-Davis, M. (2006). *Choosing a*

marital therapist. Retrieved from
http://www.divorcebusting.com/a_choosing_marital_therapist.htm

[25] Doherty, W. J. (1999). *How therapy can be hazardous to your marital health.* Retrieved from http://www.smartmarriages.com/hazardous.html; Doherty, W. J. (2002). *Bad couples therapy: How to avoid it.* Retrieved from http://www.smartmarriages.com/badcouples.doherty.html; Weiner-Davis, M. (2006). *Choosing a marital therapist.* Retrieved from http://www.divorcebusting.com/a_choosing_marital_therapist.htm; Wood, N., Crane, D., Schaalje, G., & Law, D. (2005). What works for whom: A meta-analytic review of marital and couples therapy in reference to marital distress. *American Journal of Family Therapy, 33*(4), 273–287.

[26] Bray, J., & Jouriles, E. (1995). Treatment of marital conflict and prevention of divorce. *Journal of Marital and Family Therapy, 21,* 461–473; Doherty, W. J. (2002). *Bad couples therapy: how to avoid it.* Retrieved from http://www.smartmarriages.com/badcouples.doherty.html; Gottman, J., & Silver, N. (1999). *The seven principles for making marriage work.* New York: Crown; Snyder, D., Ward, D., & McCollum, E. (2005). Treatment effectiveness and its correlates in a marriage and family therapy training clinic. *American Journal of Family Therapy, 33*(3), 207–223; Wills, R., & Grady-Fletcher, A. (1991). Long-term effectiveness of behavioral versus insight-oriented marital therapy: A 4-year follow-up study. *Journal of Consulting and Clinical Psychology. 59,* 138–141.

[27] Ward, D., & McCollum, E. (2005). Treatment effectiveness and its correlates in a marriage and family therapy training clinic. *American Journal of Family Therapy, 33*(3), 207–223.

[28] Waite, L., Browning, D., Doherty, W., Gallagher, M., Luo, Y., & Stanley, S. (2002). *Does divorce make people happy? Findings from a study of unhappy marriages.* New York: Institute for American Values.

[29] Ward, D., & McCollum, E. (2005). Treatment effectiveness and its correlates in a marriage and family therapy training clinic. *American Journal of Family Therapy, 33*(3), 207–223.

[30] Bennun, I. (1997). Relationship interventions with one partner. In W. K. Halford & H. J. Markman (Eds.), *Clinical handbook of marriage and couples interventions* (pp. 451–470). Hoboken, NJ: John Wiley & Sons.

[31] U.S. Bureau of the Census. (1993). *Marital status and living arrangements: March 1992* (Current Population Reports, Series P-20, No. 468). Washington DC: U.S. Government Printing Office.

[32] Wineberg, H. (1995). An examination of ever-divorced women who attempted a marital reconciliation before becoming divorced. *Journal of Divorce and Remarriage, 22*(3/4), 129–146.

[33] Wineberg, H. (1994). Marital reconciliation in the United States: Which couples are successful? *Journal of Marriage and the Family, 56,* 80–88.

[34] Holeman, V. T. (2003). Marital reconciliation: A long and winding road. *Journal of Psychology and Christianity, 22*(1), 30–42; Wineberg, H. (1994).

Marital reconciliation in the United States: Which couples are successful? *Journal of Marriage and the Family, 56*, 80–88.

[35] Holeman, V. T. (2003). Marital reconciliation: A long and winding road. *Journal of Psychology and Christianity, 22*(1), 30–42.

[36] Davila, J., & Bradbury, T. N. (2001). Attachment insecurity and the distinction between unhappy spouses who do and do not divorce. *Journal of Family Psychology, 15*, 371–393.

[37] Davila, J., & Bradbury, T. N. (2001). Attachment insecurity and the distinction between unhappy spouses who do and do not divorce. *Journal of Family Psychology, 15*, 371–393; Drigotas, S. M. & Rusbult, C. E. (1992). Should I stay or should I go? A dependence model of break ups. *Journal of Personality and Social Psychology. 62,* 62–87.

[38] Scharfe, E. (2003). Stability and change of attachment representations from cradle to grave. In S. M. Johnson & V. Whiffen (Eds.), *Attachment processes in couple and family therapy* (pp. 64–84). New York: Guilford Press. See also Johnson, S. (2008). *Hold me tight.* New York: Little, Brown.

[39] Davila, J., & Bradbury, T. N. (2001). Attachment insecurity and the distinction between unhappy spouses who do and do not divorce. *Journal of Family Psychology, 15*, 371–393.

[40] Furstenberg, F. F., Jr., & Cherlin, A. J. (1991). *Divided families: What happens to children when parents part.* Cambridge, MA: Harvard University.

[41] States with "time out" laws include: Maine, Ohio, Pennsylvania, and Utah.

[42] Moore, K. A., Jekielek, S. M., Bronte-Tinkew, J., Guzman, L., Ryan, S., Redd, Z. (2004). What is a "healthy marriage"? Defining the concept. *Child Trends Research Brief* (Publication #2004-16). Washington DC: Child Trends.

[43] *With this ring ... A national survey on marriage in America.* (2005). Gaithersburg, MD: National Fatherhood Initiative.

[44] Gottman, J. M., & Silver, N. (1999). *The seven principles for making marriage work.* New York: Crown.

[45] Gottman, J. M., & Silver, N. (1999). *The seven principles for making marriage work.* New York: Crown.

[46] *With this ring ... A national survey on marriage in America.* (2005). Gaithersburg, MD: The National Fatherhood Initiative.

[47] Amato, P. R., & Previti, D. (2003). People's reasons for divorcing: Gender, social class, the life course, and adjustment. *Journal of Family Issues, 24,* 602–626; Michael, R. T., Gagnon, J. H., Laumann, E. O., & Kolata, G. (1995). *Sex in America: A definitive survey.* Boston: Little, Brown; *With this ring ... A national survey on marriage in America.* (2005). Gaithersburg, MD: National Fatherhood Initiative.

[48] Michael, R. T., Gagnon, J. H., Laumann, Edward O., Kolata, G. (1995). *Sex in America: A definitive survey.* Boston: Little, Brown.

[49] Gottman, J., & Silver, N. (1999). *The seven principles for making marriage work.* New York: Crown.

[50] Amato, P. R., & Rogers, S. R. (1999). Do attitudes toward divorce affect marital quality? *Journal of Family Issues, 20,* 69–86.

[51] Waite, L. J., & Gallagher, M. (2000). *The case for marriage.* New York: Doubleday.

[52] The questions for this quiz are used with the permission of Jeffry H. Larson, Ph.D., Dean M. Busby, Ph.D., and the RELATE Institute, Brigham Young University (www.relate-institute.org). Below are references to two research studies on this and other relationship inventories: Busby, D. M., Holman, T. B., & Taniguchi, N. (2001). RELATE: Relationship evaluation of the individual, family, cultural, and couple contexts. *Family Relations, 50,* 308–316; Busby, D. M., & Loyer-Carlson, V. (2003). *Pathways to marriage: Premarital and early marital relationships.* New York: Allyn and Bacon.

Chapter 3

Does Divorce Help Adults Become Happier?

Divorce is too complex a process to produce just winners and losers. People adjust in many different ways, and these patterns of adjusting change over time.

—E. Mavis Hetherington, noted divorce researcher[1]

That was the easy part—getting the divorce. It's the aftermath that's the hard part. When you're living it, it's so magnified. It literally takes the air out of you.

—Laura

Overview: A large majority of individuals in unhappy marriages who avoid divorce end up reporting their marriages are very happy a few years later. For the most part, those who divorced and even those who divorced and remarried were not happier and better off psychologically than those who remained married. About half of all divorces come from marriages that are not experiencing high levels of conflict; individuals from these marriages generally experience a decrease in happiness over time. When individuals end high-conflict marriages, however, they usually increase their well-being over time. About two in ten individuals appear to enhance their romantic lives through their divorce, but about three in ten seem to do worse; about four in ten individuals build future romantic relationships but they have mostly the same kinds of problems as they did in their previous marriage. Divorce can eliminate some of the problems with a spouse, but it can also cause others; for many couples conflict actually increases after a divorce. Many people report having mixed feelings and even regrets about their divorce. Studies suggest some divorced individuals wished they and/or their ex-spouse had tried harder to work through their differences. About three of four divorced people will eventually remarry. However, second marriages have even higher rates of divorce, although if couples can hang on through the challenging first 5 years of remarriage, their chances for success are high.

A. Are people happier as a result of divorce?

Many people assume that the answer to the question, "Are people happier as a result of divorce?" is "yes." People thinking about a divorce may assume that it will solve a difficult problem and eventually make them happier. And sometimes it does. But studies have found that most adults are not happier when they divorce. Many different factors influence how divorce affects individuals. This chapter will review what research tells us about this complex issue.

A recent summary of research in this area found that, compared to married individuals, divorced individuals had lower levels of happiness, more psychological distress, poorer self-concepts, and felt more alone.[2] Of course, some of the poorer outcomes for divorced individuals can be explained by the unhappiness in the former marriage and the ongoing stress of divorce. Perhaps even more informative is a national study that followed happily and unhappily married individuals for a 5-year period.[3] Many of these unhappy individuals remained married, but some divorced. Those who divorced were no happier when interviewed again than those that stayed married. The study also found no differences in rates of depression, sense of mastery, or self-esteem between those who stayed married and those who divorced. This was true even if divorced individuals had remarried. For women who had experienced violence in their marriage, however, divorce did help them get away from that violence, which is important.

Another recent national study found that about half of all divorces come from marriages that were not experiencing high levels of conflict but one spouse (or both) was still unhappy.[4] When individuals ended high-conflict marriages, they increased their happiness and sense of well-being, on average. However, when individuals in a low-conflict marriage ended their marriage, they experienced a decrease in happiness, on average. This study suggests that ending a marriage that may be unhappy at the time but does not produce a high level of conflict is not a reliable path to improved happiness. One couple we know ended their low-conflict marriage because of differences about finances. Both remarried to other people. As they reflected back on their first marriage, both spouses admitted that they should have worked harder to make their first marriage work. They realized after remarrying how much hard work goes into making a good marriage. They both agreed that if they would have put the same effort into their first marriage that they are putting into their second marriages, the first marriage could have worked.

One of the best long-term studies of divorce found that divorce, in and of itself, generally does not lead to a better life.[5] These researchers found that about two in ten individuals appeared to enhance their lives, including building more satisfying romantic relationships, through divorce, but about three in ten seemed to do worse after their divorce. About four in ten individuals were able to build future romantic relationships, but they had mostly the same kinds of problems as they did in their previous marriages and didn't seem to improve their situations much. (The remaining 10% were functioning fine, but did not rebuild romantic relationships.)

It is hard to work through a difficult marriage, but it is also hard to work through a divorce. Some people are happier as a result of divorce.[6] On the other hand, many marriages that experience even very serious problems, such as alcoholism, infidelity, and emotional neglect, are now happy after working through their problems.[7] One study found that about three in ten currently married individuals in a Western state have at one time or another thought their marriage might be in serious trouble and have thought about divorce.[8] But more than 90% of these individuals said that they were glad that they were still together.

Fern and Deron are one such couple we interviewed. They struggled early in their second marriage and considered divorce. But they hung on, clinging to their commitment to each other, and worked on their problems, and years later were grateful that they did.

> We knew that we trusted each other and we knew how hard
> it is for children in the streets and in the world today. Deron
> wanted his children to be protected and cared for, and I
> wanted mine to be protected . ... It was so important for us
> not to be selfish. We knew we loved each other. The
> challenges were the life we had to deal with, and we
> weighed and measured and we both came up with the same
> decision. It's better for all concerned if two like-thinking
> people and people that love each other, even though we have
> had our rough spots—you know, he could not imagine
> himself with someone else, and I could not imagine
> myself—so we knew we would just condemn ourselves to
> being lonely, ol' angry people, and we also knew that the
> children needed both of us.

The decision to divorce may be the most difficult decision you ever face. One myth about divorce is that children will be better off because a divorce will make for happier parents. Research does not confirm that parents, on average, become happier as a result of divorce. Moreover, children are not nearly as tuned in to the quality of their parents' marriage as their parents are. If there isn't a lot of conflict in the marriage, research suggests that the children probably will be better off if their parents stay married.[9] (We will review the research about the effects of divorce on children later in Chapter 5.) Fortunately, most unhappy couples who avoid divorce will eventually be happy in their marriages again. Especially if you are currently unhappy in your marriage but not experiencing high levels of conflict with your spouse, think hard about the possibility of continuing to work to improve your relationship and being patient for things to get better. If you can do this, you and your family will probably be better off down the road. You may benefit from doing exercise 3.1, "Imagining a Happy Ending," at the end of this chapter.

B. Does conflict between spouses decrease as a result of divorce?

Some people see divorce as the cure-all; they hope that ending the marriage will be the beginning of the end of all their unhappiness. But while divorce can eliminate some problems with your spouse, it can also cause others that are very difficult to manage. It is important to remember that divorce is merely one option for solving problems in a marriage; it is not the only option and in many cases other solutions are more appropriate. Research suggests that, for many couples, conflict actually increases after a divorce and post-divorce conflict between ex-spouses makes it more difficult for children to adjust to life after the divorce.[10] Remember that most couples who divorced did not experience high levels of conflict, so the marital difficulties and unhappiness may have been hidden from the children. Divorce adds the potential for a whole new set of problems with your ex-spouse. When you are unhappy in your marriage, it's easy to underestimate how difficult the problems of un-marrying can be. Relationships don't end cleanly with divorce, only the legal status of marriage ends. Minimizing conflict with your ex-spouse after divorce is a good thing to do. But for many it is as difficult—sometimes even more difficult—than dealing with conflict while they are married. And post-divorce conflict probably is more visible to the children. Just the logistics involved with divorce—two separate residences, legal mandates, split finances, shared custody and visitation—make even the act of communicating in a clear and efficient way difficult.

We were told about one such "nightmare" divorce where one spouse would literally count the minutes of the Christmas holiday and divide it in half, subtracting out the Christmas-time visits. The inflexible spouse insisted on an exchange right to the minute. If the other spouse was even a minute late there was a big scene at the parenting exchange. This is just one example of all the demands that came from the ex-spouse. There was no flexibility about anything in the divorce settlement. The spouse was always looking for a reason to take the ex-spouse back to court. The children felt much resentment about the divorce situation and knew that any mention of the other parent would be a source of conflict. Another divorcing spouse we know expressed frustration that came when her children were looking forward to a visit from the other (noncustodial) parent and the parent never showed up or called. The hopes of the children had been dashed time and time again, yet the parent legally was entitled to every other weekend with the children. This caused a lot of conflict for the divorcing couple and they had to return to court to try and resolve issues.

Many studies have shown that conflict with an ex-spouse continues after divorce and adds a great deal of stress to life.[11] Some of the new stresses include:

❖ Your and your ex-spouse's emotional response to the divorce (e.g., anger, retaliation, resignation, acceptance, relief).

❖ Reactions of the children to the divorce.

❖ Moving households and the costs associated with it.

❖ Custody and visitation struggles.

❖ Child support payments.

❖ Financial struggles.

❖ Health problems, including greater risk for abusing drugs and alcohol.

❖ New romantic relationships or marriages that can bring both joys and headaches, happiness and sadness.

❖ Family conflicts with ex-in-laws and other family members.[12]

In all the emotional turmoil associated with an unhappy marriage, it may be hard to sort out whether conflict would decrease or increase if you divorced. A trusted religious leader and/or professional counselor may be able to help you sort your thoughts out. Also, you may benefit from doing exercise 3.2, "Thinking About Conflict After Divorce," at the end of this chapter. If your state requires you to attend a divorcing parents education class, this class also will help you find ways to minimize conflict between you and your spouse if you divorce.

C. Do some who divorce later wish they had worked harder to try to save their marriage?

This is a sensitive subject, but some recent research suggests that some people do harbor regrets about their divorces. One national expert who counsels many divorced individuals reports that ambivalent or mixed feelings about the divorce are very common.[13] In an important study that followed divorced couples over a long period of time, researchers found evidence of feelings of regret. When they interviewed individuals one year after the divorce they found that, in three out of four divorced couples, at least one partner was having second thoughts about the decision to divorce.[14] Feelings of regret decrease over time for most, as people adjust and move on. As we mentioned in Chapter 3, a handful of other surveys in various states have found that perhaps half of individuals wished they and/or their ex-spouses had tried harder to work through their differences.[15]

A recent survey of divorced individuals in a midwestern state found that 25% reported they had some regrets about getting a divorce. About 12%, or one in eight, said that looking back, they no longer were confident that they made the right decision to divorce. About one in six said that if they knew how hard things would be after the divorce, they might have worked harder to try and fix the marriage.[16]

Other research is documenting feelings of ambivalence as individuals approach divorce. One study in a (different) midwestern state found that about 25% of individuals and about 10% of couples (both spouses) going through a mandated divorcing parents class felt that their marriage could still be saved, even at that late stage in the legal process of divorce. Similarly, 30% of individuals and 10% of couples expressed interest in a formal reconciliation service, if it were available.[17]

As we interviewed people about their experiences at the crossroads of divorce, we were struck by these sentiments of regret or uncertainty, even from divorced individuals who described very serious problems in their marriage. Brittany was one such individual.

> Now that I'm older and more mature, I look back and I think, "Oh my goodness, the issues were really not as big as we made them out to be." And truly, I wish I would have done things differently to maybe work on that relationship further. Because he is a wonderful, amazing person.

Laura's thoughts on this were similar:

> The grass is not greener. … I would have done it a different way. … I would not have made the same decision. I would have worked really hard. … I would say [to others facing a decision to divorce], do not evaluate with anger because your anger is an emotion and it will guide you towards a decision that you might not be happy with down the line. I always tell people—and I have plenty of friends who … [are] having problems with their sex lives or this, that, and the other, and I say, "I don't care what it is. Figure it out. … And be extremely prayerful about it. Make sure 100% that this is not an emotion-based decision. Because when you base it off of an emotion, you're going to be sorry about the consequences later on. … Don't make these decisions based on emotion. Try to see past it. Or give yourself some time to step away. … I always steer people not to get a divorce, even though I have had one. And they always say, "Well you did it." Yeah, well, if I had a chance to go back, I probably wouldn't have done it. I tell people, "Look, if he's beating the crap out of you, we've got an issue. … But if it's about anything else, you can work through it." … People are imperfect. I know he loves me, and I was too stupid and too prideful, even though he did me wrong.

Janet, who endured nearly a decade of intense problems and marital unhappiness, almost from the first week of her marriage, surprised us with her ambivalence, even 15 years after the divorce:

> I don't think that I had a choice [about divorce]. … I have mixed feelings about that, interestingly enough. … I think right now we are better off. But the intervening 15 years were so difficult and so draining … . I think that the cost to all of us was so great, that I'm not sure we would have gotten there, you know. I think you mature and you work through things. And had we been together, I think a lot of those things would have worked themselves out. And I think it is possible we would have been better off together.

Of course, we can't say what your experience will be. And you may not have a choice in the matter. If you do have a choice, right now a divorce may look like the only solution. But these individuals' experiences suggest that you think hard about trying to repair the relationship.

One of the things we know about the divorce process is that the idea to get a divorce begins with the smallest thought deep in someone's mind. Like a seed it can be nourished and fed so that it grows and takes root. Seldom do partners talk about divorce when it is at this very early stage, or just a fleeting thought. However, this is probably the best time to be bringing up the subject to your partner. When someone has doubts about the relationship, it is almost always better to bring up the concerns rather than ignore them. Ignoring marital problems is like watering the seed of divorce. A person in discernment counseling (see Chapter 2) who was considering leaving her husband was asked, "What if you could get the same emotional support from your husband that you're getting from the man you're having an affair with?" She responded by saying, "I can't even imagine it; I've been thinking about leaving him for so long that it is difficult to think he and I could have a different type of relationship at all." She was commenting on the momentum that can build up around the idea of divorce and how her view of her marriage was very difficult to change even though now she and her husband were getting competent counseling for the first time in their marriage.

The truth of the matter is that a good marriage and a good divorce are similar in that they both require those involved to be kind and considerate to each other. Both take hard work and require each partner to bring his or her best self to the process. When the hard work is done right, the investment pays off.

D. What are my chances for remarrying and having a happy marriage?

People who divorce usually do not give up on the idea of having a happy marriage. Most of the time they want to remarry sooner or later, hoping that it will be better the next time around. Some have referred to remarriage as the triumph of hope over experience. The chances that you will marry again are good; about three of four divorced people will eventually remarry within 10 years.[18] About half who will eventually remarry have done so within 5 years.[19] There are some factors that may affect your chances of getting remarried. For example, if you have children you are less likely to remarry, probably because divorced parents struggle to find time for dating.[20] And some people aren't enthused about marrying someone with children and perhaps taking responsibilities for those children. (Research has found that women who bring children from a previous union into a second marriage face a higher risk of eventual divorce, although for some reason, this is not true for men who bring children from a previous union into a second marriage.[21]) Also, chances for remarrying decline the older you are when you divorce, probably because there are fewer single partners available at older ages.[22] However, there are still many divorced people that remarry at an older age and with children.

Unfortunately, research shows that second marriages in general are not happier or more stable. A generation ago, scholars thought that easier divorce would help to strengthen marriage. They reasoned that if people were freer to leave an unhappy marriage they could find a better match and a happier marriage. But this line of thinking appears to have been short-sighted. The divorce rate for second marriages is even higher than it is for first marriages and they break up even faster.[23] There often is more conflict in second marriages compared to first marriages. Much of this conflict comes from complications in blending families together.[24] These stresses usually subside after about 5 years. Because of this, if couples can endure these early years of remarriage, they usually find greater happiness.[25] These long-lasting remarriage relationships usually show characteristics such as friendship, support, and respect[26]—a recipe for happiness in any marriage.

Of course, bringing children into a remarriage can be very difficult for the children involved. Children in stepfamilies often experience an increase in stress, even though it probably means more financial security. The increase in stress can put children at more risk for problems. (We give more details about the challenges faced by children of divorce in Chapter 5.)

Although most people who experience a divorce will marry again, there is no guarantee that the second time around will be better. This is another reason why individuals and couples at the crossroads of divorce should think carefully and consider whether it would be better to try to repair their current relationship rather than look for another one.

Exercises for Chapter 3

3.1. Imagining a Happy Ending

A. As we discussed in this chapter, most people who are unhappy in their marriage, if they hang on for a few years, report that they are happy again. Try imagining that in 3 years both you and your spouse will be happy again in your marriage. What could happen that would explain this change for the better? Imagine a series of events, changes in circumstances, shifted attitudes, new behaviors or actions, etc., that could result in a happy marriage down the road in a few years. Be specific about the changes you would want to make in yourself and the changes you would want your spouse to make. Write down your thoughts here. If you can't imagine this scenario at all, then write down why this is the case.

_____

_____

_____

_____

_____

_____

_____

_____

_____

_____

_____

_____

_____

_____

_____

_____

_____

B. Now think what steps you and your spouse could take and changes in circumstances that could potentially turn your imaginings into reality. Write down your thoughts about this:

_____

_____

_____

_____

_____

_____

_____

_____

_____

_____

_____

_____

_____

3.2: Thinking About Conflict After Divorce

Divorce may end some conflicts you have had with your spouse, but it can also be the beginning of other conflicts. This exercise is designed to help you think about what conflicts you have had and what will happen if you divorce. Also, this exercise helps you think about what other conflicts may arise if you divorce and how challenging those conflicts may be. It might be helpful to go through this exercise with a trusted friend or counselor who may be more objective about your life than you.

Sometimes we can minimize certain realities when we're so focused on wanting a particular outcome.

A. *Current Conflicts.* What are the current conflicts you have with your spouse that cause the most difficulty and emotional pain? List those below and say how difficult the conflict is for you. Then think about whether this conflict is likely to get better (go away) or worse if you divorce, and why.

What are your most difficult conflicts in your marriage?	If you divorce, do you think the conflict will get better, worse, or stay the same?			Why? Briefly explain.
	Better	Same	Worse	
1.				
2.				
3.				
4.				
5.				

B. *Conflicts After Divorce.* Now, try to think about what conflicts you might have if you divorce that would be the most difficult and cause you the most emotional pain. These may be some of the same conflicts you currently have. But they may be new ones due to changes from divorce. List possible conflicts below. Then say how difficult you think each conflict will be. Finally, think about ways you could reduce this potential conflict.

What do you think your most difficult conflicts with your ex-spouse might be after a divorce?	How difficult do you think this conflict will be?			How could you reduce this possible conflict?
	Slightly Difficult	Somewhat Difficult	Very Difficult	
1.				
2.				
3.				
4.				
5.				

C. *Overall.* Overall, how do you think a divorce would affect conflict with your ex-spouse? Write down your thoughts here:

_____

_____

_____

_____

_____

[1] Hetherington, E. M., & Kelly, J. (2002). *For better or for worse: Divorce reconsidered.* New York: John Wiley & Sons (see p. 5).

[2] Amato, P. R. (2000). The consequences of divorce for adults and children. *Journal of Marriage and the Family, 62,* 1269–1287.

[3] Waite, L., Browning, D., Doherty, W., Gallagher, M., Luo, Y., & Stanley, S. (2002). *Does divorce make people happy? Findings from a study of unhappy marriages.* New York: Institute for American Values.

[4] Amato, P. R., & Hohmann-Marriott, B. (2007). A comparison of high- and low-distress marriages that end in divorce. *Journal of Marriage and Family, 69,* 621–638.

[5] Hetherington, E. M., & Kelly, J. (2002). *For better or for worse: Divorce reconsidered.* New York: W. W. Norton.

[6] Amato, P. R. (2000). The consequences of divorce for adults and children. *Journal of Marriage and the Family, 62,* 1269–1287.

[7] Waite, L., Browning, D., Doherty, W., Gallagher, M., Luo, Y., & Stanley, S. (2002). *Does divorce make people happy? Findings from a study of unhappy marriages.* New York: Institute for American Values.

[8] Schramm, D. G., Marshall, J. P., Harris, V. W., & George, A. (2003). *Marriage in Utah: 2003 baseline statewide survey on marriage and divorce.* Salt Lake City: Utah Department of Workforce Services (see pp. 19–20).

[9] Amato, P. R., & Booth, A. (1997). *A generation at risk.* Cambridge, MA: Harvard University.

[10] Emery, R. E., & Sbarra, D. A. (2002). Addressing separation and divorce during and after couple therapy. In A. S. Gurman & N. S. Jacobson (Eds.), *Clinical handbook of couple therapy, 3rd ed.* (pp. 508–530). New York: Guilford.

[11] Amato, P. R. (2000). The consequences of divorce for adults and children. *Journal of Marriage and the Family, 62,* 1269–1287; Sbarra, D. A., & Emery, R. E. (2005). Coparenting conflict, nonacceptance, and depression among divorced adults: Results from a 12-year follow-up study of child custody mediation using multiple imputation. *American Journal of Orthopsychiatry, 75,* 63–75.

[12] Waite, L., Browning, D., Doherty, W., Gallagher, M., Luo, Y., & Stanley, S. (2002). *Does divorce make people happy? Findings from a study of unhappy marriages.* New York: Institute for American Values.

[13] Emery, R. E., & Sbarra, D. A. (2002). Addressing separation and divorce during and after couple therapy. In A. S. Gurman & N. S. Jacobson (Eds.), *Clinical handbook of couple therapy, 3rd ed.* (pp. 508–530). New York: Guilford.

[14] Hetherington, E. M., & Kelly, J. (2002). *For better or for worse: Divorce reconsidered.* New York: W. W. Norton. See also Sbarra, D. A., & Emery, R. E. (2005). Coparenting conflict, nonacceptance, and depression among

divorced adults: Results from a 12-year follow-up study of child custody mediation using multiple imputation. *American Journal of Orthopsychiatry, 75*, 63–75.

[15] Minnesota Family Institute. (1998). *Minnesota marriage report (1998).* Minneapolis, MN: Minnesota Family Institute; New Jersey Family Policy Council. (1999). *New Jersey marriage report: An index of marital health.* Parsippany, NJ: New Jersey Family Policy Council.

[16] These figures come from unpublished data collected by David Schramm in 2012, University of Missouri Cooperative Extension Service.

[17] Doherty, W. J., Willoughby, B. J., & Peterson, B. (2011). Interest in marital reconciliation among divorcing parents. *Family Court Review, 49*, 313–321.

[18] Bramlett, M. D., & Mosher, W. D. (2001). *First marriage dissolution, divorce, and remarriage: United States.* Advanced data from vital and health statistics; no. 323. Hyattsville, MD: National Center for Health Statistics; Furstenberg, F. F., Jr., & Cherlin, A. J. (1991). *Divided families: What happens to children when parents part?* Cambridge, MA: Harvard University.

[19] Bramlett, M. D., & Mosher, W. D. (2001). *First marriage dissolution, divorce, and remarriage: United States.* Advanced data from vital and health statistics; no. 323. Hyattsville, MD: National Center for Health Statistics; Wilson, B. F., & Clarke, S. C. (1992). Remarriage: A demographic profile. *Journal of Family Issues, 13*, 123–141.

[20] Ganong, L. H., & Coleman, M. (2004). *Stepfamily relationships: Development, dynamics, and interventions.* New York: Kluwer Academic/Plenum.

[21] Teachman, J. (2008). Complex life course patterns and the risk of divorce in second marriages. *Journal of Marriage and Family, 70*, 294–305.

[22] Ganong, L. H., & Coleman, M. (2004). *Stepfamily relationships: Development, dynamics, and interventions.* New York: Kluwer Academic/Plenum (see p. 63).

[23] Bramlett, M. D., & Mosher, W. D. (2001). *First marriage dissolution, divorce, and remarriage: United States.* Advanced data from vital and health statistics; no. 323. Hyattsville, MD: National Center for Health Statistics.

[24] Coleman, M., Ganong, L., & Weaver, S. (2001). Maintenance and enhancement in remarried families. In J. Harvey & A. Wenzel (Eds.), *Close romantic relationships: Maintenance and enhancement* (pp. 255–276). Hillside, NJ: Erlbaum; Hobart, C. (1991). Conflict in remarriages. *Journal of Divorce and Remarriage, 15*, 69–86.

[25] Hetherington, E. M., & Kelly, J. (2002). *For better or for worse: Divorce reconsidered.* New York: W. W. Norton (see p. 263).

[26] Hetherington, E. M., & Kelly, J. (2002). *For better or for worse: Divorce reconsidered.* New York: W. W. Norton.

Chapter 4

How Common Is Divorce and What Are the Reasons?

Marriage is a counter-cultural act in a throwaway society.[1]

—Dr. William H. Doherty,
noted marriage scholar and therapist

Overview: In the United States, researchers estimate that 40%–50% of all first marriages and 60% of second marriages will end in divorce. There are some well-known factors that put people at higher risk for divorce: marrying at a very early age, less education and income, living together before a commitment to marriage, a premarital pregnancy, no religious affiliation, coming from a divorced family, and feelings of insecurity. The most common reasons people give for their divorce are lack of commitment, too much arguing, infidelity, marrying too young, unrealistic expectations, lack of equality in the relationship, lack of preparation for marriage, and abuse. Some of these problems can be fixed and divorce prevented. Commitment is having a long-term view of the marriage that helps us not get overwhelmed by the problems and challenges we experience day to day. When there is high commitment in a relationship, we feel safer and are willing to give more for the relationship to succeed. Commitment is clearly a factor in why some couples stay together and others divorce. Divorce is necessary at times; it may even help to preserve the moral boundaries of marriage. But parents have a responsibility to do all that they reasonably can to preserve and repair a marriage, especially when the reasons for divorce are not the most serious ones. Barriers to leaving a marriage, such as financial worries, can help keep marriages together in the short run. However, unless there is improvement in the relationship, eventually the barriers are usually not enough to keep a marriage together in the long run.

Divorce is both very personal and all too common. But there are many myths about divorce. Individuals at the crossroads of divorce may benefit by knowing the research facts about divorce rates, factors that are associated with a higher risk of divorce, and common reasons that people give for divorcing.

A. What percentage of marriages end in divorce?

In the United States, researchers estimate that 40%–50% of all first marriages will end in divorce or permanent separation.[2] The risk of divorce is even higher for second marriages, about 60%–65%.[3]

Divorce has always been present in American society.[4] Although divorce has always been a concern, it has become more common in the last 50 years. The highest divorce rates ever recorded were in the 1970s and early 1980s. Since then the divorce rate actually has decreased a little, but it still remains at a historically high rate.[5]

B. What factors are associated with a higher risk for divorce?

To say that nearly half of all first marriages end in divorce sounds a lot like saying marriage is just a game of chance. But a lot of research has identified various factors that are associated with a higher risk for divorce. So some couples actually have a low risk of divorce while others have a high risk. Understanding these factors may not directly help you improve your marriage or make a decision about divorce, but it may help you understand why you may be facing some challenges. Of course, these factors do not guarantee that you will divorce; they simply increase the risk of divorce. Here are some factors that appear to increase the risk of divorce the most. However, this should not be regarded as a complete list of risk factors.

❖ *Young age.* Marriage at a very young age increases the likelihood of divorce, especially in the early years of marriage. Those who marry in their teens have much higher divorce rates. By about age 21 or 22, however, that risk diminishes a great deal.[6] Those who delay marriage until their 20s are probably more mature and able to make marriage decisions and handle the challenges of married life better than those who marry in their teens. Waiting until the late 20s or beyond, however, does not seem to improve chances for a happier marriage.[7]

❖ *Less education.* Researchers have estimated that individuals who have some college education (vs. high school or not finishing high school) have a lower chance of divorce.[8] Apparently, investing in education is a good way to build a foundation for a better marriage, not just a better job.

❖ *Less income.* Closely related to education is income. Researchers have estimated that individuals with annual incomes of more than $50,000 have a lower chance of divorce (compared to individuals with annual incomes less than $25,000).[9] Finances can be stressful. Apparently having at least a modest income can help couples avoid some of the stresses that can lead to divorce.

❖ *Premarital cohabitation.* Couples who live together before marriage appear to have a higher chance of divorce if they marry.[10] However, this risk is mostly for those who live together with more than one partner; those who live together with one partner (whom they later marry) don't seem to be at a much greater risk for divorce.[11] In addition, research now suggests that those who get engaged before moving in together do not have a higher risk for divorce.[12] The idea that living together before marriage increases your risk for divorce goes against a lot of common beliefs that it is a good way to get to know each other better and prepare for marriage.[13] Living together may be a way to get to know each other better, but other things about living together apparently do not help—and even hurt—your chances for a successful marriage, especially if you live together with several people before marrying. Researchers have found that those who live together already have or develop more lenient attitudes about divorce. They also entangle their lives in ways that are harder to break and often end up sliding into marriage with less commitment than those who do not live together before making a strong commitment to the future.[14]

❖ *Premarital childbearing and pregnancy.* Pregnancy and childbearing prior to marriage significantly increase the likelihood of future divorce.[15] In America, more than 40% of children are born to parents who are not married,[16] and few of these parents eventually marry.[17] Most of those parents will separate before the child begins school; some will never really get together.

❖ *No religious affiliation.* Researchers have estimated that individuals who report belonging to no religious group have a somewhat higher chance of divorce than those who say they have a religious affiliation.[18] If couples share the same religious affiliation and are active in their faith together, their chances of divorce are lower.[19]

❖ *Parents' divorce.* Of course, some risk factors for divorce you can't control. If you experienced the divorce of your parents, unfortunately that doubles your risk for divorce. And if your spouse also experienced his or her parents' divorce, then your risk for divorce triples.[20] This may sound scary, but it doesn't doom your marriage to failure. It does suggest that individuals who experienced the divorce of their parents need to work even harder to make good marriage choices and to keep their marriage strong and happy. This may be good information for people to have prior to committing to marriage. Growing up in a home with marital conflict that eventually leads to a divorce can be the kind of thing that colors how a person thinks about intimate relationships. Being aware of your personal risk factors can help you to be proactive in taking care of your relationship.

❖ *Insecurity.* Researchers have found that some personality factors put people at more risk for divorce. One of the most important is feeling insecure about yourself and your self-worth. Insecure individuals are more likely to become unhappy in their marriages over time and to divorce.[21] However, even feelings of insecurity and other personality characteristics can be overcome.[22]

C. What are the most common reasons people give for their divorce?

The previous section explained what factors increase the chances of divorce. Of course, when you ask people why they got divorced they generally don't say things like, "I didn't have enough education," or "My parents were divorced." When asked this question, divorced individuals usually respond with more personal reasons.

Researchers have identified the most common reasons people give for their divorces. A national survey[23] found that the most common reason given for divorce was "lack of commitment" (73% said this was a major reason). Other significant reasons included too much arguing (56%), infidelity (55%), marrying too young (46%), unrealistic expectations (45%), lack of equality in the relationship (44%), lack of preparation for marriage (41%), and abuse (29%). (People often give more than one reason, so the percentages add up to more than 100%.) Recent surveys of adults in specific states found results similar to this national survey.[24] Looking at this list, some believe that it is possible to fix many of these problems and prevent some divorces. Couples can learn how to avoid destructive arguments and solve their differences better, they can create more realistic expectations for their marriage, and they can create more equal partnerships. Even such damaging problems as infidelity can be overcome, especially with appropriate help and support. (We discuss recovering from infidelity later in this chapter.)

Marriage counselors often talk about the differences between the "hard" and "soft" reasons for divorce. The "hard" reasons describe situations where abuse, addiction, or affairs (the 3 As) are actively happening and the person involved shows no remorse or willingness to change his or her behaviors. For example, if your partner's alcohol addiction is negatively impacting the family environment and your marriage, it needs to change for the relationship to be healthy. If the person using alcohol is not interested in or open to changing that behavior, that might be a condition where divorce could help solve a problem of a spouse who is unwilling to change. This same rationale could be applied to abuse or affairs (infidelity).

However, if there are "hard" reasons for divorce, it makes sense that there are also "soft" reasons for divorce. These include not being in or falling out of love, not sure you married the right person, just being bored with the marriage, outgrowing the relationship, being incompatible, or being such different people.

Americans marry for love. If the love is gone, or someone is not feeling it currently, then it's tempting to move out of the relationship and find new love. However, research suggests that the nature of love changes over time. The energy, excitement, and charge we feel from love at the beginning of a relationship are very different than the feelings of love that a couple might experience after years of sacrifice and dedication to one another. If you think the love is gone from your relationship, getting professional help to discover the love or redefine the love you have might be an important step in reclaiming your relationship.

It is interesting to note that a significant number of divorced individuals—maybe about half—report to researchers that they wished they or their ex-spouse had tried harder to work through their differences.[25] Researchers estimate that about one in three couples who actually divorce later try to reconcile,[26] and as we reviewed in Chapter 3, some end up having feelings of regret about their decision to divorce. You might benefit from doing exercise 4.1, "Thinking About Your Reasons For a Possible Divorce" at the end of this chapter.

D. Why is commitment so important to a successful marriage?

As we noted above, the number one reason people give for why their marriage didn't succeed is a lack of commitment on one or both spouses' parts. It may be helpful to focus on this issue of commitment. Researchers have found that about half of all divorces come from relatively low-conflict relationships.[27] Interestingly, when viewed at one point in time, these low-conflict marriages that end in divorce look very similar to happy marriages that don't end in divorce. In fact, researchers have a hard time distinguishing between these two groups of married couples except for one important factor. The difference appears to be in the level of commitment. Low-conflict individuals who are not very happy in their marriage but have higher levels of commitment to the marriage are more likely to stay together and try and make things better rather than divorce to see if they could be happier in another relationship.[28]

One prominent marriage researcher and therapist, Dr. Scott Stanley at the University of Denver, defines commitment as having a long-term view of the marriage that helps us not get overwhelmed by the problems and challenges we experience day to day. We keep our eyes focused on the valued prize—a healthy, stable marriage—and work to get there.[29]

Researchers have identified two elements of commitment.[30] The first is constraint commitment. These are things that keep us in the marriage even if things aren't going so well, for example, social pressure from family or friends, financial worries, children, religious or moral beliefs about divorce, and fear about the future. We often think about constraints as negative things in a society that values choice and freedom so highly. But constraints also can serve the purpose of keeping us from jumping ship when leaks appear in our marriage, as they always do. This is the kind of commitment Keisha was referring to in our interview as she discussed how she and her husband, Doug, were able to halt their path to divorce:

> In a way, I don't think I've ever wanted to divorce. I'd say one of the biggest goals of my life, watching my parents' [failed marriage], was to build a good marriage, so a lot of that had to do with me saying that this is really important.

When we interviewed Trisha, it was clear that constraint commitment, and in particular, concerns for how divorce would affect her children and how she would support her family, were keeping her from a divorce:

> There are periods of time where I feel like I can't do it anymore, but literally, I have stayed with him because of my kids. ... I just really feel like it would just mess up their world too much. ... If I could leave, I would leave. In fact, I think if things were a perfect situation for me now, I would still leave. So, I guess, yes, on the one hand, I stay together because of the kids, but also because, what am I going to do with five kids? And where am I going to go and how am I going to support them? ... I feel like I'm trapped a lot. But I just put on a happy face and keep going. But not because I

want to but because I feel like I'm forced, I feel like I have to, that I have no other options, at least no options that appeal to me in any way. ... Are you going to trade a marriage that you're not happy in for a really hard life of being a single mom? ... Can I just accept the way things are? It's not like I get beat up. It's not like I'm being abused in any way, other than I just feel like I have a loveless marriage, that we are just business partners. He does his thing; I do my thing to help things move along for the family. Can I accept that? I still don't know if I can accept it.

However, if this is the only kind of commitment in a marriage, then the marriage is not likely to survive long term. You might sense that from Trisha's comments. She is constantly struggling with the option of divorce. Her situation actually is unusual because she has struggled with these feelings for nearly 20 years; it's unusual for constraints like this to hold a marriage together that long without developing a second, stronger form of commitment: personal dedication. This involves a real desire to be together with one's spouse in the future, a sense of "we-ness," or an identity as a couple, not just two individuals. It also involves making the relationship and the spouse a priority, and a willingness to sacrifice for the spouse. It also means making the choice to give up other choices, so we stay focused on our spouse and on our marriage rather than wondering about other possibilities. When there is high dedication commitment in a relationship, we feel safer and are willing to give more for the relationship to succeed. Personal dedication is the kind of commitment that was saving Keisha and Doug's marriage:

> *Keisha:* I changed my focus from, "Should we get a divorce?" to "Okay, we've been through all these hard things and we've made it through. I sure hope it doesn't keep going like this, but we're going to keep trying and this is a challenge that is worth taking up."

> *Doug:* What we decided was that from here on out this is our marriage now, and we're going to be committed to each other. And we had to lay that foundation again, because it felt like something was broken.

When commitment seems to be fading, it can be helpful to remember the good times in the relationship and to talk about your dreams for the future together. You may benefit from doing Exercise 4.2, "Thinking About Commitment in My Marriage," at the end of this chapter.

E. Are there clearly valid reasons for divorce? Are abuse, infidelity, or addictions valid reasons?

Research can provide important facts, but research alone can't answer questions of moral judgment. Most Americans (70%) believe that divorce, in general, is a morally acceptable choice.[31] And many feel that divorce is a personal, private matter and that it is their choice alone whether or not to divorce. Legally, this is correct. Some individuals may feel that a few months of arguments and disappointments justifies their divorce, while other couples will stay together even through infidelity and abuse. In our opinion, it is important for the law to allow the option of divorce. Divorce actually protects and highlights the moral boundaries around marriage. There are circumstances and behaviors that clearly violate those boundaries. Individuals have the right to be physically and emotionally safe in a relationship. And society has the right to try to protect the moral boundaries of marriage to preserve the integrity of such an important private and social institution. The stakes are even higher when children are involved. because those children also have a stake in the marriage but a much smaller voice in marital decision making. And society has a stake in the well-being of the next generation. As we will discuss in Chapter 5, family breakdown puts children at greater risk for many serious problems. Most children are better off when their parents can resolve their difficulties and keep the family together. (Of course, our current laws allow one spouse to end a marriage at any time for any reason without the agreement of the other spouse. So many times a divorce is not a choice for an individual but an unwelcome fact.)

While we believe that divorce is necessary and right at times, we also believe that parents have a heavy responsibility to do all that they reasonably can to preserve and repair a marriage. This is especially true when the reasons for divorce are not the most serious ones. We don't think this is a radical perspective to hold about divorce. In fact, public opinion polls suggest that nearly half of Americans (43%) agree that, in the absence of violence and extreme conflict, parents who have an unsatisfactory marriage should stay together.[32] But when individuals are deeply unhappy in their marriages, for whatever reasons, it is only natural in our society to wonder if things wouldn't be better for everyone if the marriage were ended. In some circumstances, we believe—and research supports—that divorce is the better option. In other circumstances, we believe—and again research supports—that the best option for all would be to repair the relationship and keep the family together, if possible.

What you believe about divorce, however, is more important to your circumstances than what we believe. You may benefit from doing Exercise 4.3, "Personal Philosophy About Divorce," at the end of the chapter.

Abuse in Marriages. Abuse in marriages deserves special consideration. As we said earlier, there are behaviors that are clearly outside the moral boundaries of marriage. And all have the right to be safe—physically, emotionally, and sexually—in their marriages. This includes adults and children. In our interview with Vera, we learned of her decision to end a marriage when she found out that two of her children were being abused by their father:

> Two of my children came to me and told me their father had sexually abused them. At that moment I was done. That night I made sure my children were not at home—I worked nights—and the next day I confronted him and told him he no longer lived with us. … He was very angry. "You can't do this to me. What do you think you're doing? You can't do this on your own. I didn't do anything. I don't know what you're thinking." He made several comments like that over time, and I finally just lost it and got right in his face. He'd never seen me lose my temper like that. "Who do you think you are? You are done." And I told him explicitly what I knew (about the abuse). … It was absolutely the right decision (to divorce). There was no other option.

Vera reported in our interview that her children, though still dealing with the long-term problems of being sexually abused, were in better shape because she terminated the marriage. When there is abuse in a marriage or in a family, not surprisingly there is evidence that ending the marriage may be best for all involved. Abused wives who divorce usually are better off than those who remain in this unsafe relationship.[33] Also, children whose parents are in a high-conflict or abusive marriage generally are better off if their parents divorce than if they stay married.[34] And boys who view violence in their families growing up are much more likely to become abusive in their personal relationships as adults.[35] One of the unfortunate facts of family life is that severe abuse seldom corrects itself. So leaving an abusive situation, although difficult and sometimes even dangerous, is probably the right thing to do for the family.

One thing to note, however, is that researchers are learning that there are at least two different kinds of relationship violence: "situational couple violence" and "intimate partner terrorism."[36] Usually when we talk about abuse we mean the latter. Intimate partner terrorism is about domination and control of one spouse by the other. It is almost always men who are guilty of this kind of abuse. These men often have a need for power and control. Some also struggle with controlling their impulses and often have hostile feelings towards women in general. Intimate partner terrorism can be physical or psychological control. It can be sexual force. (Many states have a law against marital rape.) It can involve severe economic control, such as not allowing a wife to have access to any money. Sometimes it involves almost completely isolating a wife from her family and friends. And sadly, this kind of abuse usually gets worse and more severe over time. If you are the victim of this kind of abuse, seek help. You probably will need to end the marriage.

On the other hand, there is a different kind of abuse in intimate relationships called "situational couple violence." Any kind of aggression or violence in a relationship is unhealthy and can harm adults and children. But situational couple violence is not as severe and dangerous as intimate partner terrorism. It involves things like pushing, shoving, kicking, slapping, shouting, name-calling, etc., and it appears that it does not escalate to more severe aggression.[37] Situational couple violence often comes when someone is experiencing a lot of stress about something. Men and women appear to do it in equal amounts, although men do more damage and their aggression tends to create fear in the relationship.[38] This abuse seems to be more about ineffective problem-solving skills rather than power or control. And as people get older this kind of abuse usually decreases, suggesting that immaturity is a factor. Thus, as people become more mature and as they learn better problem-solving skills, this kind of aggression appears to decrease. If this kind of aggression exists in your marriage, you and your spouse can learn to solve your problems more effectively. As you do so, and as violence is eliminated, you may be able to avoid divorce. (See Chapter 2 about resources to improve your problem-solving skills and relationship.)

You may want to look at Box 4.1, "Signs of Abuse." Also, you may benefit from doing Exercise 4.4, "Is There Abuse in My Marriage?" at the end of this chapter. There are resources and services for victims of domestic abuse in many states. And in some states you can simply call 211 for a list of community services in your area.

One final thought to consider about abuse. Some people think that because there is a risk of abuse in marriage, they won't marry. But research shows that married individuals are much less likely to experience abuse than unmarried individuals living together or dating, even when taking account of other differences between these two groups of people, such as education and income.[39] So when people are in romantic relationships, marriage is the safest relationship.

Box 4.1: Signs of Abuse

(from the National Domestic Violence Hotline
http://www.ndvh.org/educate/what_is_dv.html)

You may be in an emotionally abusive relationship if your partner:

- ❖ Calls you names, insults you, or continually criticizes you.
- ❖ Does not trust you and acts jealous or possessive.
- ❖ Tries to isolate you from family or friends.
- ❖ Monitors where you go, who you call, and who you spend time with.
- ❖ Does not want you to work outside the home.
- ❖ Controls finances or refuses to share money.
- ❖ Punishes you by withholding affection.
- ❖ Expects you to ask permission.
- ❖ Threatens to hurt you, the children, your family, or your pets.
- ❖ Humiliates you in any way.

You may be in a physically abusive relationship if your partner has ever:

- ❖ Damaged property when angry (thrown objects, punched walls, kicked doors, etc.).
- ❖ Pushed, slapped, bitten, kicked, or choked you.
- ❖ Abandoned you in a dangerous or unfamiliar place.
- ❖ Scared you by driving recklessly.
- ❖ Used a weapon to threaten or hurt you.
- ❖ Forced you to leave your home.
- ❖ Trapped you in your home or kept you from leaving.
- ❖ Prevented you from calling police or seeking medical attention.
- ❖ Hurt your children.
- ❖ Used physical force in sexual situations.

You may be in a sexually abusive relationship if your partner:

❖ Views women as objects and believes in rigid gender roles.

❖ Accuses you of cheating or is often jealous of your outside relationships.

❖ Wants you to dress in a sexual way.

❖ Insults you in sexual ways or calls you sexual names.

❖ Has ever forced or manipulated you into to having sex or performing sexual acts.

❖ Held you down during sex.

❖ Demanded sex when you were sick, tired, or after beating you.

❖ Hurt you with weapons or objects during sex.

❖ Involved other people in sexual activities with you.

Infidelity in Marriage. Unfortunately, too many couples face the challenge of infidelity; that is, one or both spouses have been sexually unfaithful. Infidelity is one of the leading causes of divorce; it nearly doubles the chance that a couple will get divorced.[40] And even though we live in a sexually tolerant society, still more than 90% of Americans say infidelity is morally wrong.[41] Although it is hard to do research on how common infidelity is, about 5% of married men and 4% of married women report anonymously to researchers that they were unfaithful to their spouses in the last year. Although most married people appear to be faithful, research suggests that about 10% of women and 20% of men tell researchers that they were unfaithful to their spouse while they were married.[42] Of course, it's possible the actual numbers are somewhat higher than this.

The discovery of infidelity is usually traumatic and recovering from infidelity is difficult.[43] Therapists who help couples deal with infidelity describe three stages in the process of recovering from infidelity:[44] (1) absorbing and dealing with the traumatic impact of infidelity; (2) creating meaning for why the affair occurred; and (3) moving forward with one's life—either together or apart—with this new understanding. In the first stage, individuals find that their whole world seems to be upside down. They may struggle to function with day-to-day life. They struggle to go on with life when something so fundamental in their life is broken. They have to find ways to absorb this change and still function. Next, they have to find understanding and meaning about the infidelity. They need to know why it happened. And then they need to explore ways to recover and rebuild trust and intimacy. To do this, they need to find some level of safety and security again in the relationship. Then they need to develop a realistic and balanced view of their relationship, including the positives and the negatives. They need to find a way to let go of the negative emotions connected with the infidelity. The injured spouse needs to voluntarily let go of her or his desire to punish the participating partner. Often the offending spouse has to find a way to let go of his or her guilt. And finally, they need to evaluate carefully their relationship and reach healthy decisions about whether to stay together and keep working to improve the relationship or to separate.

Opinion polls show that nearly two out of three (63%) married Americans say they would not forgive their spouse (and would get a divorce) if they found out their spouse had a sexual affair.[45] This was the case for Fran. She found out about her husband's infidelity when she discovered she had contracted a venereal disease:

> I decided when I found out on the hospital table that I had gonorrhea that we were divorced already. ... He tried to talk me out of it, and so did his mother and his father, and my mother, and various aunts and uncles and brothers and sisters, but I was very willful and stubborn, and I would not be appeased. I was furious [about his infidelity]. The marriage was over, personally.

Many couples who have dealt with infidelity in their marriages, however, find the will and the strength to stay together. Researchers have found that while most people say they would get a divorce if they discovered their spouse was unfaithful, in actuality, 50%–60% of married couples who experience infidelity stay together.[46] Brittany described the difficult choice she faced at one point. She decided to work hard and try to repair the damage to her marriage:

> I had to make a decision: Am I willing to work through this situation [infidelity] with him which is going to be a long-term thing? And how will that impact me for the rest of my life? How am I going to feel about us? How am I going to trust again? Can I love him with all of my heart again? I'm telling you, that's a hard, hard, hard, hard thing. Harder than I ever thought. Because even though it's been a few years, still, you seem to doubt. ... In my head I thought, "I love these kids so much, and I want them to have [their parents] together for the rest of our lives." Marriage is a lot of work, and people don't realize that.

A few years later, she told us that she is happy in her marriage and is sure she made the right decision to stay and work things out. An excellent resource to learn more about recovering from marital infidelity is the book, *Getting Past the Affair: A Program to Help You Cope, Heal, and Move On—Together or Apart.*[47] Also, you should seriously consider getting help from a well-trained marriage counselor and/or a dedicated religious leader who will help you with the hard work of healing, deciding what to do, and repairing the marriage, if you decide to stay together.

Addictions in Marriage. Another difficult problem that can cause people to seriously consider divorce is addiction. One woman we know was stunned when she discovered her husband was addicted to drugs. The drugs led to crime and she was devastated as the story unfolded. But she was determined to fight for her family, especially her two children. The couple separated for a time and after some rehabilitation for the husband and support groups for the wife the family was able to come back together. The addicted spouse had an amazing turnaround in his life and the family has been flourishing for several years now. Unfortunately, this family's experience may not be the norm.

In recent years, addiction to pornography has become a challenge to many marriages. Early research suggests that cybersex addictions are a major factor contributing to separation and divorce for many couples.[48] Many women view pornography as a form of infidelity.[49] The Internet is used by more than half of Americans and 20%–30% of those people who use the Internet use it for sexual purposes.[50] The majority of people who have sexual addictions involving Internet pornography are married, heterosexual males.[51] Not surprisingly, early research on pornography and marital relationships has found that frequent pornography use tends to be associated with sexually aggressive behavior, sexual deviance, decreased intimacy, decreased sexual satisfaction, and increased marital dissatisfaction.[52] One woman we know decided to divorce after she realized the seriousness of the pornography issues her husband faced. Yet another woman decided to support and help her husband through his addiction. It was a long and arduous path that included having a candid talk about the pornography use, working with a church leader, using support groups, regularly initiating conversation about pornography issues for both the husband and the wife, monitoring computer use, and having tight filters and passwords. This woman feels it was worth the effort. Each person has unique circumstances and must decide what is right for her or him.

F. How do individuals decide to divorce or remain married?

Researchers have found that individuals considering divorce make their decision to stay or leave based on the rewards they gain from the marriage, the barriers against leaving the marriage, their perceptions about finding a better relationship, and the amount of investment they have made in their marriage.[53] Some individuals decide to stay together, even if the rewards from marriage are currently low, when there are important barriers to divorce, such as concerns about money, the effects of family breakup on their children, religious beliefs about the importance of marriage, disapproval from family and friends, or fears of being single again.[54] Similarly, some will decide to stay with the marriage if they don't think their prospects for a better relationship are good. Also, if individuals have invested many years in a marriage, have children together and a home and other possessions, then they are more hesitant to leave.[55]

All of this sounds very rational. But research also is beginning to show that people making the decision to divorce are usually emotional, unsure, confused, and feel lost and disoriented. Thus it can take a long time to make a decision. Most seem to understand that these feelings of confusion are inevitable.[56] One person who considered divorce but decided to stay married compared her recurring thoughts of divorcing to someone who, during times of stress, thinks about hurting him or her self, but makes no specific plans to do so. Moving away from the decision to divorce has been described as a long and gradual process.[57]

As we mentioned earlier, barriers to leaving a marriage can keep marriages together in the short run. However, unless there is improvement in the relationship, eventually the barriers are usually not enough to keep a marriage together in the long run.[58] Eventually, the rewards of a healthy and happy marriage—love, friendship, and a shared life—are the stronger glue that keeps couples together.

Exercises for Chapter 4

4.1. Thinking About Your Reasons for a Possible Divorce

A. Below are some of the more common reasons people give for divorce. Consider what role each of these reasons plays in your situation. Circle whether each reason is a major problem, a minor problem (and may have you thinking about a divorce) or not a problem in your marriage. (If something is a problem for your spouse but not for you, go ahead and circle what you think your spouse would say.) Then for each reason you checked, take a minute to think about how willing you and your spouse would be to work to make improvements in this area. (Chapter 2 discussed different ways to work to make improvements in your relationship.)

Reason for Divorce/ Problem in Marriage	Is this a major reason, a minor reason, or not a reason for thinking about a divorce? (circle one)	How willing would you be to work on making improvements in this area? How willing do you think your spouse would be? 1 = Not at all willing 2 = A little willing 3 = Somewhat willing 4 = Very willing n/a = Not applicable in your situation (circle one)
Lack of commitment	major / minor / not	You: 1 2 3 4 n/a Spouse: 1 2 3 4 n/a
Too much arguing	major / minor / not	You: 1 2 3 4 n/a Spouse: 1 2 3 4 n/a
Infidelity (unfaithful)	major / minor / not	You: 1 2 3 4 n/a Spouse: 1 2 3 4 n/a
Unrealistic expectations	major / minor / not	You: 1 2 3 4 n/a Spouse: 1 2 3 4 n/a
Lack of equality	major / minor / not	You: 1 2 3 4 n/a Spouse: 1 2 3 4 n/a
Pushing, slapping, yelling, etc.	major / minor / not	You: 1 2 3 4 n/a Spouse: 1 2 3 4 n/a
Abuse	major / minor / not	You: 1 2 3 4 n/a Spouse: 1 2 3 4 n/a
Didn't prepare well for marriage	major / minor / not	(Not applicable)
Married too young	major / minor / not	(Not applicable)
Other: _____	major / minor / not	You: 1 2 3 4 n/a Spouse: 1 2 3 4 n/a

4.2. Thinking About Commitment in My Marriage

As we discussed in this chapter, there are two elements of commitment: constraint and personal dedication. Constraint commitment includes those things that keep you in a marriage, even if things aren't going well, like financial worries or concerns about how a divorce might affect your children. In the long run, however, constraint commitment is usually not enough to hold a marriage together; dedication commitment is needed. Dedication commitment is a real desire to be with your spouse, to build a life and a future together, and a willingness to sacrifice for each other. Consider your situation and both elements of commitment and write down your thoughts.

A. *Constraints Against Divorce.* Think about each of the following and whether it would be a big constraint, a little constraint, or not a constraint against divorce (circle your answer). Then briefly write why it might hold you back from a divorce.

Possible Divorce Constraint	3 = Big 2 = Little 1 = Not a Concern (circle one)	Why?
1. Fear it would hurt my children.	3 2 1	
2. Fear my spouse wouldn't stay involved with the children.	3 2 1	
3. Fear my children would lose contact with extended family members (e.g., spouse's parents).	3 2 1	
4. Financial worries (money would be tight).	3 2 1	
5. Might lose our home and have to move.	3 2 1	
6. Not sure if I could get a good job to support the family.	3 2 1	
7. I might lose health insurance or other benefits from my spouse's job.	3 2 1	

Possible Divorce Constraint	3 = Big 2 = Little 1 = Not a Concern (circle one)	Why?
8. My spouse might not pay regular child support.	3 2 1	
9. Fear of what family or friends might think if I get a divorce.	3 2 1	
10. It will feel like a personal failure.	3 2 1	
11. Religious concerns (disapproval of divorce).	3 2 1	
12. Uncertainty about what the future holds for me.	3 2 1	
13. Fear of ever finding another love.	3 2 1	
14. Don't want to have to date again.	3 2 1	
15. Fear that arguments with my spouse will get worse if we divorce.	3 2 1	
16. Fear of getting abused if I try to get a divorce.	3 2 1	
17. Other:	3 2 1	
18. Other:	3 2 1	
19. Other:	3 2 1	
20. Other:	3 2 1	

Now, stop and think about your responses. What have you learned about the constraints that may or may not hold you back from getting a divorce? Write down a few thoughts.

_____

_____

B. *Dedication Commitment.* Next, think about your situation and dedication commitment. Even though you may be having some serious problems, how dedicated are you to your spouse? Answer these questions as honestly as possible by circling the number that best describes you. (These questions were developed by prominent researchers who study commitment in relationships.[59])

Dedication Item	Strongly Disagree	Disagree	Somewhat Disagree	Neither Agree nor Disagree	Somewhat Agree	Agree	Strongly Agree
1. I don't make important commitments unless I will keep them.	1	2	3	4	5	6	7
2. My relationship with my spouse is more important to me than anything else.	1	2	3	4	5	6	7
3. I want this relationship to stay strong no matter what rough times we may encounter.	1	2	3	4	5	6	7
4. I like to think of my spouse and me more in terms of "us" and "we" than "me" and "him/her."	1	2	3	4	5	6	7
5. My marriage to my spouse is clearly part of my future plans.	1	2	3	4	5	6	7
6. It makes me feel good to sacrifice for my partner.	1	2	3	4	5	6	7

7. I want to have a strong identity as a couple with my spouse.	1	2	3	4	5	6	7
8. I want to be with my spouse a few years from now.	1	2	3	4	5	6	7
9. I am not seriously attracted to anyone else right now.	1	2	3	4	5	6	7
10. I do not think about what it would be like to be with someone else (romantically).	1	2	3	4	5	6	7

Now score your dedication commitment by adding up the numbers you circled. Your score: _____

❖ If your score is **higher than 50**, you are probably dedicated and committed to your spouse, even if you are having serious problems at this time.

❖ If your score is **50 or less but more than 30**, then you are probably struggling somewhat with dedication and commitment in your marriage at this time.

❖ If your score is **30 or less**, then you are probably not dedicated and committed to your spouse at this time.

C. *Increasing Your Commitment.* How can you increase your commitment? One way to increase your dedication commitment is to remember the good times and all the good things you have gone through together. When you are going through hard times, it is so easy to forget these good things. Write your answer to each of these questions.

1. What attracted you to your spouse at first and then later on?

_____

_____

_____

2. What are 2–3 of the happiest times in your marriage? Why?

_____

_____

_____

3. What are 2–3 of the most difficult times in your marriage that you have been able to overcome?

_____

_____

_____

_____

4. What 2–3 important values do you feel you still have in common with your spouse?

_____

_____

_____

5. What 2–3 important goals do you feel you still share with your spouse?

_____

_____

_____

6. What would be the biggest loss if you got divorced?

_____

_____

_____

7. What would be the biggest gain if you can stay together?

_____

_____

_____

8. What three things could you do to increase your dedication commitment and show more loyalty to your spouse? Write them down here.

A. _____

B. _____

C. _____

D. *Your Spouse's Commitment.* You have been thinking about your commitment to your marriage and your spouse. Obviously, your spouse's commitment to you is equally important. Low commitment from either spouse can make it hard to stay together. But if both are committed, your chances of solving your problems and keeping your marriage together are much better. Take a few minutes now and think about how your spouse might answer the questions in this exercise, "Thinking About Commitment in My Marriage." Of course, this can be hard to do. It's hard to know exactly what your spouse is feeling and thinking. But it may be helpful to try to honestly assess your spouse's commitment. What constraints would be on his/her list? How would he/she score on dedication commitment? How would he/she answer the questions above in part C? What have you learned by thinking about commitment from your spouse's perspective? Write down your thoughts here:

_____

_____

_____

_____

_____

E. *Putting It All Together.* Considering all the information in this exercise, what do you think about continuing to try and work out the challenges in your relationship? Write down your thoughts here:

_____

_____

_____

_____

_____

4.3. Personal Philosophy About Divorce

When two people get married, they usually aren't thinking that the marriage will end in divorce. But then hard times arise and sometimes they find themselves thinking either casually or seriously about divorce. But most people haven't really thought carefully about their philosophy of divorce. When, if ever, is it justified? How hard and how long should people try to work things out? Does it make a difference if they have children? Does it matter how old the children are? There are many things to consider, but many people haven't clarified the answers to these questions. This exercise will invite you to do this. Thinking about marriage and divorce in general (not your marriage specifically), answer these questions as honestly as you can.

A. What circumstances do you think could justify divorce?

_____

_____

_____

_____

_____

_____

B. What circumstances do you think do *not* justify divorce?

_____

_____

_____

_____

_____

C. If the married couple has children, does that affect your answers in A and B above? Do the ages of the children matter?

_____

_____

_____

_____

_____

D. How long do you think a married couple should try to work things out? Does your answer to this question depend on some of the circumstances you wrote about above?

_____

_____

_____

_____

_____

E. What steps do you think people should take before deciding to get divorced? (For instance, get counseling.)

_____

_____

_____

_____

_____

F. Why do think you have these beliefs? What has shaped your beliefs? (For instance, religious principles, family experiences growing up, friends you have observed going through a divorce, your ideological or political views.)

_____

_____

_____

_____

_____

G. Now apply this personal philosophy to your circumstances. How does your personal philosophy guide your thinking about the challenges you are facing in your marriage? What does this mean in terms of thinking about divorce? Write your thoughts here:

_____

_____

_____

_____

_____

_____

Of course, as we have acknowledged many times, your spouse may have a different philosophy and it only takes one person to end a marriage. If it helps, you may want to try and think how your spouse would answer these questions.

4.4. Is There Abuse in My Marriage?

As we discussed in this chapter, there are at least two kinds of violence: "situational couple violence" and "intimate partner terrorism." Situational couple violence involves things like pushing, shoving, kicking, yelling, etc., and is done by men and women equally, although men generally do more damage than women. When there is situational couple violence in a relationship, the couple needs to improve their communication and problem-solving skills. (Part B of this exercise will help you see if there is this kind of abuse in your marriage.) A second kind of abuse, intimate partner terrorism, is more serious. It involves more severe forms of physical, emotional, and sexual violence, and is done to control the other person. This kind of violence is almost always done by men against women.

A. *Assessing Intimate Partner Terrorism.*[60] This questionnaire can help you judge whether there is intimate partner terrorism in your marriage, a very serious and dangerous form of violence in a relationship. For each question, circle the number that best represents your relationship. Then add up your scores.

My Spouse...	Never	Rarely	Sometimes	Often	Almost Always
1. Makes me feel like I'm walking on eggshells to keep the peace	0	1	2	3	4
2. Keeps me away from family and friends	0	1	2	3	4
3. Yells at me often, and calls me names	0	1	2	3	4
4. Doesn't care about my needs and expectations	0	1	2	3	4
5. Is unpredictable or has sudden mood swings	0	1	2	3	4
6. Puts me down, to look better	0	1	2	3	4
7. Retaliates when I disagree	0	1	2	3	4
8. Breaks or hits things in my presence	0	1	2	3	4

My Spouse...	Never	Rarely	Sometimes	Often	Almost Always
9. Is forceful with things like affection and/or sex	0	1	2	3	4
10. Controls all the money and gives me little or none	0	1	2	3	4
11. Is possessive of me, or jealous of me	0	1	2	3	4
12. Sometimes physically hurts me	0	1	2	3	4
Add up your TOTAL SCORE:					

Compare your score to these categories:
* ❖ 0–19 = little risk of abuse
* ❖ 20–30 = likelihood of minor abuse
* ❖ 31 and higher = likelihood of serious abuse

If your score is higher than 31:
* ❖ It is a good idea to get help (see http://www.ncadv.org/ or a local agency).
* ❖ Also, individual counseling, rather than couples' counseling, is probably best.

B. *Assessing Situational Couple Violence.*[61] This questionnaire can help you judge whether there is situational couple violence in your marriage, such as slapping and pushing. Although this kind of physical aggression in marriage is not as serious as intimate partner terrorism, it is still an indication of some unhealthy parts in a marriage.

No matter how well a couple gets along, there are times when they disagree on decisions, get annoyed about something the other person does, or have arguments or fights because they are in a bad mood or for some other reason. A couple may also use many different ways to settle their differences. Below are some things that you or your partner may have done when you had a disagreement or fight. For each question, circle the answer that best represents what *your spouse* has done. Next, answer the same questions about what *you* have done.

Thinking about your spouse, during the past 12 months . . .							
1. How many times, if any, has your spouse hit you?	0	1	2	3–5	6–10	11–20	20+
2. How many times has your spouse twisted your arm or hair?	0	1	2	3-5	6–10	11–20	20+
3. How many times has your spouse pushed, shoved, or kicked you?	0	1	2	3-5	6–10	11–20	20+
4. How many times has your spouse grabbed you forcefully?	0	1	2	3-5	6–10	11–20	20+
5. How many times has your spouse slapped you?	0	1	2	3-5	6–10	11–20	20+
Now, thinking about yourself, during the past 12 months . . .							
6. How many times, if any, have you hit your spouse?	0	1	2	3-5	6–10	11–20	20+
7. How many times have you twisted your spouse's arm or hair?	0	1	2	3-5	6–10	11–20	20+
8. How many times have you pushed, shoved, or kicked your spouse?	0	1	2	3-5	6–10	11–20	20+
9. How many times have you grabbed your spouse forcefully?	0	1	2	3-5	6–10	11–20	20+
10. How many times have you slapped your spouse?	0	1	2	3-5	6–10	11–20	20+

There is no scale that says how much of this behavior in a relationship is acceptable or how much is too much. Any behavior like this in a marriage is unhealthy and indicates a need to improve your communication and problem-solving skills.

❖ Looking over your answers, what have you learned about situational couple violence in your marriage? Have you and your spouse been able to avoid these kinds of behaviors? If so, this is a strength in your relationship. Or do you and your spouse sometimes use these ineffective and unhealthy ways to deal with disagreement and problems? If so, do both of you behave this way sometimes, which is more common, or is it just one of you? Write down your thoughts here:

_____

_____

_____

_____

_____

_____

_____

❖ If you and/or your spouse sometimes use these ineffective and unhealthy ways to deal with disagreements and problems, how can you improve your ability to discuss things and solve disagreements in a healthier way? You may want to consider some of the marriage education resources suggested in Ch. 2 to improve your communication and problem-solving skills. Write down your thoughts and plans here:

_____

_____

_____

_____

Endnotes to Chapter 4

[1] Retrieved from www.uuworld.org/2005/01/feature3.html

[2] Popenoe, D., & Whitehead, B. D. (2007). The state of our unions 2007: The social health of marriage in America. Piscataway, NJ: National Marriage Project (see pp. 18–19).

[3] Bramlett, M. D., & Mosher, W. D. (2002). Cohabitation, marriage, divorce, and remarriage in the United States. *Vital and Health Statistics, 23*(22). Hyattsville, MD: National Center for Health Statistics.

[4] Amato, P. R., & Irving, S. (2006). Historical trends in divorce in the United States. In M. A. Fine & J. Harvey (Eds.), *Handbook of divorce and relationship dissolution*. Mahwah, NJ: Lawrence Erlbaum Associates.

[5] Popenoe, D., & Whitehead, B. D. (2007). *The state of our unions 2007: The social health of marriage in America*. Piscataway, NJ: National Marriage Project (see pp. 18–19).

[6] Bramlett, M. D., & Mosher, W. D. (2002). Cohabitation, marriage, divorce, and remarriage in the United States. *Vital and Health Statistics, 23*(22). Hyattsville, MD: National Center for Health Statistics; Heaton, T. B. (2002). Factors contributing to increased marital stability in the United States. *Journal of Family Issues, 23*, 392–409; White, L. K. (1990). Determinants of divorce: A review of research in the eighties. *Journal of Marriage and the Family, 52*, 906–908.

[7] Hymowitz, K., Carroll, J. S., Wilcox, W. B., & Kaye, K. (2013). *Knot yet: The benefits and costs of delayed marriage in America*. Washington, DC: National Campaign to Prevent Teen and Unplanned Pregnancy, RELATE Institute, & National Marriage Project.

[8] Bramlett, M. D., & Mosher, W. D. (2002). Cohabitation, marriage, divorce, and remarriage in the United States. *Vital and Health Statistics, 23*(22). Hyattsville, MD: National Center for Health Statistics.

[9] Bramlett, M. D., & Mosher, W. D. (2002). Cohabitation, marriage, divorce, and remarriage in the United States. *Vital and Health Statistics, 23*(22). Hyattsville, MD: National Center for Health Statistics.

[10] Jose, A., O'Leary, D., & Moyer, A. (2010). Does premarital cohabitation predict subsequent marital stability and marital quality? *Journal of Marriage and Family, 72*, 105-116; Bramlett, M. D., & Mosher, W. D. (2002). Cohabitation, marriage, divorce, and remarriage in the United States. *Vital and Health Statistics, 23*(22). Hyattsville, MD: National Center for Health Statistics; White, L. K. (1990). Determinants of divorce: A review of research in the eighties. *Journal of Marriage and the Family, 52*, 906–908.

[11] Lichter, D. T., & Qian, Z. (2008). Serial cohabitation and the marital life course. *Journal of Marriage and Family, 70*, 861–878.

[12] Rhoades, G. K., Stanley, S. M., & Markman, H. J. (2009a). The pre-engagement cohabitation effect: A replication and extension of previous

findings. *Journal of Family Psychology, 23*, 107–111; Rhoades, G. K., Stanley, S. M., & Markman, H. J. (2009b). Working with cohabitation in relationship education and therapy. *Journal of Couple & Relationship Therapy, 8*, 95–112.

[13] Popenoe, D., & Whitehead, B. D. (2002). Should we live together? What young adults need to know about cohabitation before marriage: A comprehensive review of recent research. Piscataway, NJ: National Marriage Project.

[14] Rhoades, G. K., Stanley, S. M., & Markman, H. J. (2009a). The pre-engagement cohabitation effect: A replication and extension of previous findings. *Journal of Family Psychology, 23*, 107–111; Rhoades, G. K., Stanley, S. M., & Markman, H. J. (2009b). Working with cohabitation in relationship education and therapy. *Journal of Couple & Relationship Therapy, 8*, 95–112; Stanley, S. M. (2005). *The power of commitment.* San Francisco: Jossey-Bass; Stanley, S. M., Whitton, S. W., & Markman, H. J. (2004). Maybe I do: Interpersonal commitment and premarital or nonmarital cohabitation. *Journal of Family Issues, 25*, 496–519.

[15] Bramlett, M. D., & Mosher, W. D. (2002). Cohabitation, marriage, divorce, and remarriage in the United States. *Vital and Health Statistics, 23*(22). Hyattsville, MD: National Center for Health Statistics; White, L. K. (1990). Determinants of divorce: A review of research in the eighties. *Journal of Marriage and the Family, 52*, 906–908.

[16] Cherlin, A. J. (2009). *The marriage-go-round.* New York: Knopff; Mincieli, L., Manlove, J., McGarrett, M., Moore, K., & Ryan, S. (2007). The relationship context of births outside of marriage: The rise of cohabitation. *Child Trends Research Brief* (Publication #2007-13). Washington DC: Child Trends.

[17] Bendheim-Thoman Center for Research on Child Wellbeing. (2003). Union formation and dissolution in fragile families. *Fragile Families Research Brief* (July 2002, Number 9). Princeton, NJ: Princeton University; Cherlin, A. J. (2009). *The marriage-go-round.* New York: Knopf.

[18] Bramlett, M. D., & Mosher, W. D. (2002). Cohabitation, marriage, divorce, and remarriage in the United States. *Vital and Health Statistics, 23*(22). Hyattsville, MD: National Center for Health Statistics.

[19] Call, V. A., & Heaton, T. B. (1997). Religious influence on marital stability. *Journal for the Scientific Study of Religion, 36*, 382–392; Lehrer, E. L., & Chiswick, C. U. (1993). Religion as determinant of marital stability. *Demography, 30*, 385–403; Stark, R. (2012). *America's blessings: How religion benefits everyone, including atheists.* West Conshohocken, PA: Tempelton Press.

[20] White, L. K. (1990). Determinants of divorce: A review of research in the eighties. *Journal of Marriage and the Family, 52*, 906–908; Wolfinger, N. H. (2005). *Understanding the divorce cycle: The children of divorce in their own marriages.* New York: Cambridge University.

[21] Davila, J., & Bradbury, T. N. (2001). Attachment insecurity and the distinction between unhappy spouses who do and do not divorce. *Journal of Family Psychology, 15*, 371–393.

[22] Davila, J., & Bradbury, T. N. (2001). Attachment insecurity and the distinction between unhappy spouses who do and do not divorce. *Journal of Family Psychology, 15*, 371–393; Scharfe, E. (2003). Stability and change of attachment representations from cradle to grave. In S. M. Johnson & V. Whiffen (Eds.), *Attachment processes in couple and family therapy* (pp.64–84). New York: Guilford Press.

[23] *With this ring ... A national survey on marriage in America.* (2005). Gaithersburg, MD: National Fatherhood Initiative.

[24] Johnson, C. A., Stanley, S. M., Glenn, N. D., Amato, P. R., Nock, S. L., Markman, H. J., & Dion, M. R. (2002). *Marriage in Oklahoma: 2001 baseline statewide survey on marriage and divorce.* Stillwater, OK: Oklahoma State University Bureau for Social Research; Schramm, D. G., Marshall, J. P., Harris, V. W., George, A. (2003). *Marriage in Utah: 2003 baseline statewide survey on marriage and divorce.* Salt Lake City: Utah Department of Workforce Services (see p. 26).

[25] Minnesota Family Institute. (1998). *Minnesota marriage report (1998).* Minneapolis: Minnesota Family Institute; New Jersey Family Policy Council. (1999). *New Jersey marriage report: An index of marital health.* Parsippany: New Jersey Family Policy Council.

[26] Wineberg, H. (1995). An examination of ever-divorced women who attempted a marital reconciliation before becoming divorced. *Journal of Divorce and Remarriage, 22*(3/4), 129–146.

[27] Amato, P. R. & Hohmann-Marriott, B. (2007). A comparison of high-and low-distress marriages that end in divorce. *Journal of Marriage and Family, 69*, 621–638.

[28] Amato, P. R. & Hohmann-Marriott, B. (2007). A comparison of high-and low-distress marriages that end in divorce. *Journal of Marriage and Family, 69*, 621–638.

[29] Stanley, S. M. (2005). *The power of commitment: A guide to active lifelong love.* San Francisco: Jossey-Bass.

[30] Stanley, S. M. (2005). *The power of commitment: A guide to active lifelong love.* San Francisco: Jossey-Bass.

[31] Saad, L. (2008, May 19). Cultural tolerance for divorce grows to 70%. *Gallup Poll.* Retrieved from www.gallup.com/poll/107380/Cultural-Tolerance-Divorce-Grows-70.aspx

[32] *With this ring ... A national survey on marriage in America.* (2005). Gaithersburg, MD: National Fatherhood Initiative.

[33] Amato, P. R., & Booth, A. (1997). *A generation at risk.* Cambridge, MA: Harvard University; Hetherington, E. M., & Kelly, J. (2002). *For better or for worse: Divorce reconsidered.* New York: W.W Norton.

[34] Amato, P. R., & Booth, A. (1997). *A generation at risk.* Cambridge, MA: Harvard University.

[35] Holtworth-Munroe, A., & Stuart, G. L. (1994). Typologies of male batterers: Three subtypes and the differences among them. *Psychological Bulletin, 116,* 476–497.

[36] Holtworth-Munroe, A., & Stuart, G. L. (1994). Typologies of male batterers: Three subtypes and the differences among them. *Psychological Bulletin, 116,* 476–497; Johnson, M. P. (1995). Patriarchal terrorism and common couple violence: Two forms of violence against women. *Journal of Marriage and the Family, 57,* 283–294; Johnson, M. P., & Ferraro, K. J. (2000). Research on domestic violence in the 1990s: Making distinctions. *Journal of Marriage and the Family, 62,* 948–963; Johnson, M. P., & Leone, J. M. (2005). The differential effects of intimate terrorism and situational couple violence: Findings from the National Violence Against Women Survey. *Journal of Family Issues, 26,* 322–349.

[37] Holtworth-Munroe, A., & Stuart, G. L. (1994). Typologies of male batterers: Three subtypes and the differences among them. *Psychological Bulletin, 116,* 476–497; Johnson, M. P. (1995). Patriarchal terrorism and common couple violence: Two forms of violence against women. *Journal of Marriage and the Family, 57,* 283–294.

[38] Johnson, M. P. (1995). Patriarchal terrorism and common couple violence: Two forms of violence against women. *Journal of Marriage and the Family, 57,* 283–294.

[39] Brown, S. L., & Bulanda, J. R. (2008). Relationship violence in young adulthood: A comparison of daters, cohabitors, and marrieds. *Social Science Research, 37,* 73–87; Waite, L. J., & Gallagher, M. (2000). *The case for marriage.* New York: Doubleday.

[40] Amato, P. R., & Previti, D. (2003). People's reasons for divorcing: Gender, social class, the life course, and adjustment. *Journal of Family Issues, 24,* 602–626; Atkins, David, personal communication, May 21, 2008; this statistic is based on an unpublished analysis of General Social Survey data, 1991–2002.

[41] Saad, L. (2008, May 19). Cultural tolerance for divorce grows to 70%. *Gallup Poll.* Retrieved from www.gallup.com/poll/107380/Cultural-Tolerance-Divorce-Grows-70.aspx

[42] Laumann, E. O., Gagnon, J. H., Michael, R. T., & Michaels, S. (1994). *The social organization of sexuality.* University of Chicago; Michael, R. T., Gagnon, J. H., Laumann, E. O., & Kolata, G. (1995). *Sex in America: A definitive survey.* Boston: Little, Brown; *The truth about American marriage.* Public opinion poll conducted by Insight Express, June, 2008; see www.parade.com/hot-topics/2008/09/truth-about-american-marriage-poll-results

[43] Baucom, D. H., Snyder, D. K., & Gordon, K. C. (2008). *Treating infidelity: An integrative approach to resolving trauma and promoting forgiveness.* New York: Guilford Press.

[44] Baucom, D. H., Snyder, D. K., & Gordon, K. C. (2008). *Treating infidelity: An integrative approach to resolving trauma and promoting forgiveness.* New York: Guilford Press.

[45] Jones, J. M. (2008, March 25). Most Americans not willing to forgive unfaithful spouse. *Gallup Poll.* Retrieved from www.gallup.com/poll/105682/Most-Americans-Willing-Forgive-Unfaithful-Spouse.aspx

[46] Atkins, David, personal communication, May 21, 2008; this statistic is based on an unpublished analysis of General Social Survey data, 1991–2002.

[47] Snyder, D. K., Baucom, D. H., & Gordon, K. C. (2007). *Getting past the affair: A program to help you cope, heal, and move on—together or apart.* New York: Guilford.

[48] Manning, J. C. (2006). The impact of internet pornography on marriage and the family: A review of the research. *Sexual Addiction and Compulsivity, 13*(2–3), 131–165.

[49] Manning, J. C. (2006). The impact of internet pornography on marriage and the family: A review of the research. *Sexual Addiction and Compulsivity, 13*(2–3), 131–165.

[50] Manning, J. C. (2006). The impact of internet pornography on marriage and the family: A review of the research. *Sexual Addiction and Compulsivity, 13*(2–3), 131–165.

[51] Manning, J. C. (2006). The impact of internet pornography on marriage and the family: A review of the research. *Sexual Addiction and Compulsivity, 13*(2–3), 131–165.

[52] Manning, J. C. (2006). The impact of internet pornography on marriage and the family: A review of the research. *Sexual Addiction and Compulsivity, 13*(2–3), 131–165.

[53] Heaton, T. B. & Albrecht, S. L. (1991). Stable unhappy marriages. *Journal of Marriage and the Family, 53,* 747–758; Knoester, C., & Booth, A. (2000). Barriers to divorce: When are they effective? When are they not? *Journal of Family Issues, 21,* 78–99; Previti, D. & Amato, P. R. (2003). Why stay married? Rewards, barriers and marital stability. *Journal of Marriage and the Family, 65,* 561–573.

[54] Heaton, T. B., & Albrecht, S. L. (1991). Stable unhappy marriages. *Journal of Marriage and the Family, 53,* 747–758; Previti, D. & Amato, P. R. (2003). Why stay married? Rewards, barriers and marital stability. *Journal of Marriage and the Family, 65,* 561–573.

[55] Davila, J., & Bradbury, T. N. (2001). Attachment insecurity and the distinction between unhappy spouses who do and do not divorce. *Journal of Family Psychology, 15,* 371–393.

[56] Fackrell, T. A. (2012). *Wandering in the wilderness: A grounded theory study of the divorce or reconciliation decision-making process.* Unpublished doctoral dissertation, Brigham Young University.

[57] Kanewischer, E. J. W. (2012). *Deciding not to un-do the "I do": A qualitative study of the therapy experiences of women who consider divorce but decide to remain married.* Unpublished doctoral dissertation, University of Minnesota.

[57] Doherty, W. J. (1999). *How therapy can be hazardous to your marital health.* Retrieved from http://www.smartmarriages.com/hazardous.html

[58] Knoester, C., & Booth, A. (2000). Barriers to divorce: When are they effective? When are they not? *Journal of Family Issues, 21,* 78–99.

[59] Stanley, S. M., & Markman, H. J. (1992). Assessing commitment in personal relationships. *Journal of Marriage and the Family, 54,* 595–608; Stanley, S. M., Whitton, S. W., & Markman, H. J. (2004). Maybe I do: Interpersonal commitment and premarital or nonmarital cohabitation. *Journal of Family Issues, 25,* 496–519.

[60] Adapted from the National Coalition Against Violence and from the Intimate Justice Scale. See Jory, B. (2004). The Intimate Justice Scale: An instrument to screen for psychological abuse and physical violence in clinical practice. *Journal of Marital and Family Therapy, 30,* 29–44.

[61] This exercise was adapted from a domestic violence screening questionnaire created by the Relationship Research Institute. We thank Dr. John Gottman for his assistance.

Chapter 5

What Are the Possible Consequences of Divorce for Children?

Divorce is a life-transforming experience. After divorce, childhood is different. Adolescence is different. Adulthood—with the decision to marry or not and have children or not—is different. Whether the outcome is good or bad, the whole trajectory of an individual's life is profoundly altered by the divorce experience.

—Dr. Judith S. Wallerstein, noted divorce researcher[1]

Overview: Divorce generally puts children at two to three times greater risk for many kinds of problems. Despite the greater risk, however, most children of divorce do not experience those serious problems; most children are resilient, and most have returned to a pretty normal life after two to three years. The problems children of divorce may experience are often present even before the divorce, perhaps the result of conflict between parents, less attention from parents, depression, or other factors. Children in a high-conflict marriage situation generally are better off if their parents decide to divorce compared to children whose parents stay married and continue to experience high levels of conflict. Children in low-conflict marriage situations, however, generally do worse when their parents divorce compared to children whose parents stay married and keep trying to work things out. Children are developing physically, socially, emotionally, educationally, morally, and spiritually; research shows that divorce can affect children in each of these developmental areas. In adulthood, children of divorce are two to three times more likely to experience a divorce compared to children who did not experience their parents' divorce.

When thinking about the possibility of a divorce, one of the most important things that people think about is how divorce will affect their children. Janet told us in our interview with her how central this concern had been to her:

My children would cry every time Daddy left the house
[while we were separating]. They would just be sobbing and
crying for Daddy, and I would be holding them. And of
course I wanted the marriage to work. And it was very
difficult. What was difficult was to watch it hurting them and
then not being able to do anything about that; to bring this
pain into my children's life and not be able to stop that,
because you are the guardian and caretaker of children.

It would be nice if we could provide you with a simple,
straightforward answer to whether divorce will be harmful to your
children. In one survey of more than 2,000 California adults, two out of
three divorced Californians said their divorce negatively impacted their
children in some way.[2] Overall, good research over many years does find
that children who experience the divorce of their parents are at higher
risk for a wide range of negative consequences, usually two to three
times the risk compared to children who do not go through a divorce.
The best circumstance for children is a stable home with two parents who
are happy and in a healthy relationship. If an unhappy marriage can be
repaired and restored to a condition of health so that both partners can be
reasonably happy, this will probably be the best situation for the
children. If, however, a divorce is necessary, it is important to know what
research says about how divorce affects children. In this chapter we
briefly summarize what we know from a large body of good research
about the effects of family breakdown on children.

A. Why are some children more affected by divorce than others?

People rightly worry about the harm to children of divorce. But
things are more complicated than a simple assertion of harm. First,
although divorce generally puts children at greater risk for many kinds of
problems, most children do not experience those serious problems, even
though the experience of divorce is personally painful for almost all
children. It turns out that children generally are strong and resilient. And
research suggests that even though divorce can be very upsetting to
children, most adjust to their new life after two to three years.[3] Of course,
this is a general statement; some children are not as resilient as others
and are more likely to be affected negatively by the divorce. And even
resilient children report long-term challenges. In one study of young
adults attending a prestigious university who had experienced a divorce
growing up but were generally well adjusted, half still said that they
worried about big events, such as graduation and weddings, when both
parents would be present. Similarly, nearly half felt that they had a

harder childhood than most and that their parents' divorce still caused struggles for them. More than a quarter wondered if their father even loved them.[4]

A second complicating factor is that the problems children of divorce may experience are certainly not just the result of a divorce. That is, the problems children of divorce may experience are often present even before the divorce, perhaps because of conflict between parents, less attention from parents, a parent's depression, or other factors. So divorce may just be an obvious target to blame when the bigger problem is that the children were experiencing the problems of their parents' unhappiness and associated problems. On the other hand, for many children, conflict between parents increases after divorce rather than decreases. So in some instances the actual divorce is the source of more difficulties and contention for children.

One child of divorce we know expressed his gratitude that his parents had never made him choose one parent over the other. His parents were able to talk through their problems and make a decision for the benefit of their child. He was grateful that he was not put in the middle. Another child of divorce we know had a very different experience; the parents forced each child in the family to make a decision when they were 10 years old on which parent they would live with. This was very difficult for the children. Still another individual we know grew up in a family with a marriage that was very rocky due to addictions. He felt his success in life was the direct product of the tremendous sacrifices his mother made. He and his siblings are very grateful that their mother and father worked through their difficult issues. All of the children in this family now have healthy marriages.

Life is complicated, circumstances are unique, and individuals are different, so there are no easy answers to the question of how divorce may affect children. But good research has been able to provide some general clues that can help you understand how divorce *might* affect your children. Here are a couple of important factors to consider.

High-Conflict vs. Low-Conflict Marriage. In earlier chapters, we explained that half or more of all divorces come from marriages that were not experiencing high levels of conflict. In high-conflict marriages, conflicts and problems are probably visible to all members of the family, including children. In a high-conflict marriage there is yelling, screaming, and throwing things; sometimes there is even more severe violence and abuse. But in a low-conflict marriage in which one or both spouses are unhappy, the problems are usually not so public and noticeable; marital problems are more private and children are unlikely to know that anything is seriously wrong. Research suggests that children in a high-conflict marriage are actually better off, on average, if their parents decide to divorce, compared to children whose parents stay married and continue to experience high levels of conflict.[5] These children almost expect or even sometimes hope that their parents will decide to separate. But this is probably not the case for children in low-conflict marriages. These children generally do somewhat worse when their parents divorce compared to children whose parents stay married and keep trying to work things out. In many situations, these children are not aware of their parents' unhappiness and the discovery that their parents are divorcing and the family is breaking up can be devastating. It is important to note that different children may have their own perceptions of their parents' marriage, and a divorce can be devastating in any situation.[6] But the children who seem to be hardest hit by divorce are those whose parents weren't having a lot of conflict. As we discussed earlier in Chapter 2, if you are in a low-conflict but unhappy marriage, there may be ways to make your marriage happy and healthy again. If this is possible, this will probably be best for your children. If you are in a high-conflict marriage, your children are probably aware of your problems and your unhappiness, especially if they are older; they may better understand that a divorce is needed to make life better for them and you.

Resilient vs. At-Risk Children. One of the foremost researchers on the effects of divorce described children's experience of divorce this way: "For a young child, psychologically, divorce is the equivalent of lifting a hundred-pound weight over the head. Processing all the radical and unprecedented changes—loss of a parent, loss of a home, of friends—stretches immature cognitive and emotional abilities to the absolute limit and sometimes beyond that limit."[7] Some children are stronger or more resilient than others. Less resilient children are those most likely not to adjust well to all the stresses and changes and losses that usually accompany divorce. So consider carefully characteristics in your children that might indicate that they will have a harder time adjusting to the divorce. For instance, research suggests that a child's temperament makes a difference in how a child adapts to stressful situations, such as divorce. If a child is agreeable and adapts easily to different situations, then she or he usually adjusts better to divorce. Similarly, if a child has good social skills—warm with others, understanding of others and their feelings, uses humor, etc.—then he or she usually adapts better.[8]

Parenting Behavior. Children's characteristics can make a difference in how they adjust to divorce, but research suggests that the quality of parenting they receive is probably the most important factor. Unfortunately, because of all the stresses in their lives, divorcing parents are less likely to be effective in their parenting, to be harsher or more permissive. Janet was very honest about this with us in her interview:

> And you're just such a … wreck [right after the divorce]; you're just such a wreck for your kids, and for everyone. … I lived with my parents [when I first got divorced]. … But it was a little hard because … little kids of divorce are usually poorly behaved, and there is a lot of compensating, and you're just so exhausted. You don't always have consistent discipline and love and everything.

One teenage girl we know confided that her parents had put her in the middle of their divorce. Her mother inappropriately confided in this young girl about many of her relationship problems. This stripped her of the carefree innocence she once had. The girl began to fail in school and felt burdened by her parents' expectations that she take messages back and forth and smooth conflicts between her divorced parents. Another couple we know divorced in a very friendly way and did it without using attorneys. Unfortunately, as soon as one of the spouses remarried, 6 months later, they regularly ended up calling in the police to resolve their fights at parent-time exchanges.

So as hard as it can be, you need to make good parenting a high priority in your life, regardless of whether you stay together or get a divorce. Some do a very good job of this. One couple we know decided after the divorce to make cooperative parenting their top priority. They were able to be very flexible in the way they used their parent time. They both came to all of the children's activities and were able to have an active life raising their children together but in different households. They were able to have monthly parenting meetings and communicate well regarding any issues with their children.

Box 5.1 has suggestions for good books to read about the effects of divorce on children and effective parenting after divorce.

If you divorce and have children, many states now require you to participate in a class designed to help with parenting after divorce. Classes like this can help parents be more sensitive to their children's needs after divorce.[9]

> **Box 5.1: Recommended Books About the Effects of Divorce on Children and Effective Parenting After Divorce**
>
> • *For Better or Worse: Divorce Reconsidered, Surprising Results from the Most Comprehensive Study of Divorce in America,* by E. Mavis Hetherington and John Kelly. New York: W.W. Norton, 2002.
>
> • *The Unexpected Legacy of Divorce: A 25-year Landmark Study,* by Judith S. Wallerstein, Julia M. Lewis, and Sandra Blakeslee. New York: Hyperion, 2000.
>
> • *The Truth about Children and Divorce: Dealing with the Emotions So You and Your Children Can Thrive,* by Robert E. Emery. New York: Viking Press, 2004.

A large body of research provides strong evidence that conflict between parents negatively affects their children's well-being.[10] Whether the parents stay married or divorce, it is important to minimize conflict. Many parents who struggle with marital conflict and divorce give their children less attention and may even reject or withdraw from their children.[11] Parents experiencing marital conflict tend to use harsher and more inconsistent discipline[12] and have more conflict with their children.[13] These negative parenting behaviors likely explain a great deal of the emotional, behavioral, social, and health problems some children experience after divorce.[14]

If parents maintain warm and positive relationships with their children, they lower the risk that their children will suffer these negative consequences.[15] Using consistent, appropriate discipline for misbehavior, such as setting appropriate limits and consequences,[16] can also help reduce misbehavior and other problems children may experience.[17] A specific technique that can help children deal with the stress of marital conflict or divorce is "emotion coaching," which is helping your child become aware of his or her emotions and talking about and acting on them appropriately.[18] When children use this skill, they can avoid many of the negative outcomes associated with marital conflict.[19] Emotion coaching also can help parents handle their own emotions better and be less hostile in marital conflict. A book that can teach you this valuable skill of emotion coaching is *The Heart of Parenting: Raising an Emotionally Intelligent Child,* by Dr. John M. Gottman (with Joan DeClaire. New York: Fireside, 1997). In addition, you may benefit from doing Exercise 5.1, "How Well Might My Children Adjust to Divorce?" at the end of the chapter.

We have been discussing the effects of divorce as if effects were one general thing. But they are actually many different things. The process of family disruption marked by divorce can affect children in many developmental areas. Next we summarize the research on the effects of divorce on children's specific developmental areas.

B. What are the possible social, emotional, and physical health consequences of divorce?

While many children grow up leading healthy and productive lives after a divorce occurs, they are at greater risk for emotional and physical problems. Some children are more emotionally affected by divorce than others. But some do not experience serious, long-term emotional problems.

Persistent feelings of loneliness are common in children of divorce.[20] One study found that nearly half (44%) of children of divorce many years later said, "I was alone a lot as a child," compared to only about one in seven children from intact families.[21] That loneliness comes in several ways. It's common for children to "lose" a parent, usually the father, from divorce. While many fathers try to stay actively involved in the lives of their children, research shows that after a couple of years most fathers—maybe as many as 70%—do not have much contact with their children.[22] Of course, if mothers are working more (or get involved in dating again) after the divorce then children may feel a loss of time with their mothers, as well.[23] Perhaps the loss of time with fathers and mothers explains that, later in life, adult children of divorce are about 40% less likely to say they see either their mother or father at least several times a week, and they rate their current relationships with both mother and father less positively than do children from intact marriages.[24] Children of divorce also can lose contact with grandparents.[25] Also, it is common for children to have to move when their parents divorce. This can result in a loss of friendships that contributes to children's feelings of loneliness.[26]

A child's emotional security also becomes more fragile during this difficult time of divorce. Fears that both parents will abandon the child are common. Depending on the age of the child, some of the ways a child might express this emotional insecurity may be:

❖ large amounts of anger, directed both toward others and themselves

❖ frequent breaking of rules

❖ sleep problems

- ❖ defying parents or teachers
- ❖ frequent guilt
- ❖ increasing isolation or withdrawal from friends and family
- ❖ drug and/or alcohol abuse
- ❖ early sexual activity
- ❖ thoughts of suicide or violence

Many young children of divorce believe that they caused the divorce or that they did something wrong that made one or both parents not want to be with them. These feelings can cause a child to feel sad, depressed, and angry.[27] These negative emotions can contribute to other problems, such as poor health, difficulty in school, and problems with friends, to name a few. Parents can help their children avoid some of the negative consequences of these emotions by using emotion coaching, as we discussed earlier in the chapter.

Children who experience the divorce of their parents generally are more likely to struggle socially compared to children from intact families. They are more likely to be aggressive, have poorer relationships with same-age children, and have fewer close friends.[28] Also, these children and teenagers appear to be less involved in extracurricular activities, such as sports or music, and other enrichment programs, such as after-school classes or summer programs. This is likely due to less money to pay for such activities, less availability of parents to drive the child and attend lessons and events, more frequent moves, and visiting and custody schedules that interrupt participation in team sports and other activities.[29]

Children and teenagers who experience the divorce of their parents may end up getting less parental supervision. As a result, some scholars believe that these children may be more susceptible to the influence of their peers and this increases the chances of them getting involved in deviant behavior, including drug and alcohol use and smoking.[30]

One such family we know had problems with their daughter's anorexia following divorce. Along with the eating disorder, the daughter got involved with drugs. The father, who had primary custody of the girl, worked hard to help her through these difficult issues and used many resources such as counseling and parent–teen mediation. Not surprisingly, there was ongoing conflict between the ex-spouses about the daughter. Another family we know had troubles with their son for several years after the divorce with depression and severe truancy issues.

Parenting children requires much cooperation between parents, whether the parents are together or divorced.

In addition, some scholars believe that some children of divorce are less likely to learn crucial social skills in the home, such as cooperation, negotiation, and compromise, that are necessary for success in life.[31] Children exposed to high levels of conflict between their parents, both before and after a divorce, may learn to model the poor communication of their parents. Children exposed to consistent, intense conflict between parents are more likely to develop lasting expectations of conflict. This can increase the likelihood of conflict in their own personal relationships as children and even as adults, which may make forming stable, satisfying relationships as adults more challenging.[32] Of course, some children vow not to repeat the mistakes they saw their parents make when they grow up.

Generally, research has not found large differences in how boys and girls tend to adjust to divorce. However, it seems that boys, more than girls, tend to be more aggressive toward others and this can lead to their friends and peers rejecting them.[33] Boys may be somewhat more likely to act in defiant ways at home and in school; girls may be somewhat more likely to experience anxiety and depression.[34] A child's age when his or her parents divorce is another factor that parents worry about. But overall, research on how a child's age might increase or decrease the effects of divorce on children has not shown a consistent pattern.[35] That is, there are challenges within any age group of children that experience a divorce, although the specific problems might differ for younger or older children.

Although these risks for children of divorce that researchers have found may seem overwhelming, most children and families do overcome them and adjust fairly well a few years after the initial crisis period of the family breakup. Remember, every child responds differently to a divorce, and though divorce does put them at greater risk of emotional and social problems, these problems are not inevitable.[36]

Given the added stresses of a family breaking up, it's not surprising that children of divorce experience more physical health problems. Children living with both biological parents have better health than children of divorce.[37] Children of divorce are more likely to experience injury, asthma, and headaches than children from intact families.[38] Following divorce, children are more likely to develop health problems than children living continuously in two-parent families.[39]

Many of the physical symptoms experienced by children of divorce are caused by their increased anxiety, stress, and emotional insecurity. Children of divorce sometimes lose health insurance coverage, as well. As a result of these health problems, some research has even found that children who experience a divorce will end up living fewer years.[40]

C. What are the possible educational consequences of divorce?

Another area of children's lives that may be at risk as a result of divorce is academics. Children of divorced parents perform more poorly in school and have less academic success than children of intact families. However in most studies, these differences are modest rather than large.[41] Fewer children of divorce graduate from high school, however.[42] About 10% fewer children go on to college if their parents are divorced and they are about 30% less likely to receive their college degree compared to children of married parents.[43]

The reasons for these modest differences in education are pretty straightforward. Academic performance may suffer if a child is experiencing stress or acting rebelliously as a result of parental conflict and divorce. Parents may be less able to carefully monitor the child's performance in school or help with homework because they may have less time and energy to devote to their children.[44] In addition, divorced parents are less able to afford private lessons, educational toys, books, home computers, and other goods for their children that may facilitate academic success. More financial strains may also force families to live in neighborhoods in which school programs are poorly financed and services are inadequate.[45]

Also, financial strains may limit parents' ability to help their children go on to college. Many children of divorce do not set goals for college because they don't think that financial support from parents will be available.[46] If they do go to college, many children of divorce complain that they do not get financial help.[47] This was the case for one very bright and ultimately successful woman we know. She put herself through college working various jobs, eating baked potatoes and carrots, and depriving herself of sleep for four years. She got a little support from her mother, who was also struggling to survive financially, and none from her estranged father. Even decades later she gets emotional recalling that lack of support and those hard times in college. She also feels that some problems with her health may be a result of poor nutrition and sleep and constant stress during her college years.

Again, however, remember that most of the differences in academic performance of children of divorce are modest, not large. Individual children respond differently to divorce; many may not struggle in their academic performance and achievement.

D. What are the possible religious and spiritual consequences of divorce?

Along with the emotional, social, physical, and academic risks that divorce brings to children, many parents worry about the effects on children's religious beliefs and behavior. Until recently, not much research was done on this question and there is still much to be discovered in this area. A recent national study compared young adults who grew up with divorced parents with young adults whose parents stayed married. It found that those who grew up in divorced families considered themselves spiritual about as often as those from intact families, but they were less likely to consider themselves religious. They attended church less often than those whose parents did not divorce; those who did attend were less likely to be a member at that place of worship.[48] In addition, this study found that almost twice as many children of divorce believed they could find ultimate truth without help from a religion and many felt that religion didn't address the important issues in their lives. Another interesting finding was that these children were also more than twice as likely to doubt their parents' religious beliefs.[49]

One possible reason for a decline in these children's religious behavior could be the disruption in family church attendance as a result of divorce. Those in divorced families attended church less regularly and felt less encouragement from their parents to practice a religious faith.[50]

In many states, "standard visitation" in divorce cases requires that children spend every other Saturday and Sunday, the two most common days for congregational services, with the noncustodial parent. This can be a struggle for couples regardless of their religious denomination. In one family we know, the children were bounced back and forth on alternate weekends as required by court order. One parent become less active in religious services and would not take the children to church on his weekends despite his ex-wife's pleading. On a positive note, we know of many divorcing couples who work out a plan for their children's religious activity. This requires them to be flexible enough to work around activities and events held by church youth groups.

Another reason for the decline in the religious activity of children of divorce could be that they feel a lack of compassion from people in the church they attend.[51] Also, perhaps it is more difficult for children of divorce to believe in a caring God because of the lack of trust and anger they have had toward their parents. One girl expressed her struggle this way: "Faith? Faith in what? What am I going to believe in? I believed my parents were going to be there. ... Now what do I believe in? I don't want to deal with what-ifs or promises or dreams."[52] Many children have similar feelings. In the study we mentioned earlier, one in five children of divorce agreed that it is hard to believe in a God who cares when they think about all the bad things that have happened in their life. Although many have a hard time with faith and belonging to a particular religion or congregation, there are also some who turn to God for comfort. About four in ten children of divorce think of God as "the loving father or parent [they] never had in real life."[53] The biggest factor in children's religious involvement, however, is their parents' religious involvement.

E. What are the possible consequences of divorce for children's sexual behavior?

A divorce can bring more stress and loneliness for children. Children may lose the active presence of a parent. They are likely to see their parents dating again and even share a home with a parent's unmarried romantic partner. Unfortunately, research confirms that children of divorce are more likely to engage in sexual behavior at earlier ages and to become pregnant (or get someone pregnant).[54] One important reason for this finding is that divorced parents are often less effective at monitoring their teenage children; poorer monitoring of teens is associated with earlier sexual activity and pregnancy.[55]

Research also shows that the quality of parenting is important to helping teenagers avoid early sexual activity and pregnancy, even more important than whether a family is divorced or intact.[56] But divorce can reduce a parent's ability to be effective. For instance, it's important to be consistent as a parent, and divorced parents struggle with this for various reasons. Inconsistent parenting contributes to greater sexual risk for teens.[57]

F. What are the possible consequences of divorce for children's future adult romantic relationships? What are the odds of divorce for children of divorce?

Parents at the crossroads of divorce also sometimes worry that their example of divorce will hurt their children's chances of building a healthy, stable, life-long marriage. Unfortunately, research does confirm that children who experience the divorce of their parents are at greater risk for a divorce when they eventually marry. One important national study found that marriages in which one spouse comes from a divorced family are about twice as likely to dissolve as marriages in which neither spouse comes from a divorced family.[58] Moreover, those marriages where both the husband and wife experienced the divorce of their parents growing up are almost three times more likely to end in divorce than marriages where both spouses come from intact families. And children of divorce are more likely than children from intact families to marry someone who also had this same experience. These risks for divorce are even higher if the children's parents ended a low-conflict marriage rather than a high-conflict marriage.

Why is there a greater risk for children to divorce if their parents divorce? There are probably many reasons. First of all, there are differences between children whose parents divorce and children whose parents do not. For instance, they have fewer financial resources and tend to have less education. They also tend to marry younger. But even when these differences are accounted for by researchers, there are specific reasons for the greater risk. One of the most important reasons that researchers have identified is that children of divorce, in general, seem to have less commitment to the ideal of lifelong marriage than children from intact marriages.[59] Put another way, experiencing your parents' divorce tends to undermine your faith in marital permanence, so you are more likely to leave an unsatisfying relationship than hang in and try to improve it. In addition, other research suggests that children of divorce have greater difficulty trusting people, including a spouse.[60] Perhaps for these reasons, children of divorce are more likely to live with a boyfriend or girlfriend before making a decision to marry. However, research shows that living together before marriage, or cohabiting, is not an effective way to increase your odds of success in marriage, and it may even increase the chances of eventual divorce.[61] However, if couples are engaged before they begin living together, they do not seem to have a higher risk for divorce.[62]

5.1: How Well Might My Children Adjust to Divorce?

It's important to consider how a divorce may affect your children. Divorce is generally a stressful experience for all children, but certain factors can make divorce harder or easier for children to deal with. As you answer these questions, keep in mind the personalities and characteristics of your children. Whether you divorce or not, answering these questions can help you better understand your children's needs at this time.

A. *Children's Perspectives*. In this chapter, you learned that children tend to have a more difficult time adjusting to divorce when their parents have a low-conflict marriage. On the other hand, in general, children tend to benefit from divorce when their parents had a high-conflict marriage. Either way, it is important to consider how your children experience your marriage. How do you think your children view your marriage? For each of these questions, circle the answer that best describes your situation.

	Unsure/ Not Applicable	Never	Rarely	Sometimes	Often	Very Often
1. My children see or hear our marital conflict.	Unsure/ NA	0	1	2	3	4
2. My children are aware of the topics of conflict between me and my spouse.	Unsure/ NA	0	1	2	3	4
3. My children get involved in our marital conflict.	Unsure/ NA	0	1	2	3	4
4. My children see violence between me and my spouse.	Unsure/ NA	0	1	2	3	4
5. My children act scared, hide, or leave home (or want to leave home) during our marital conflict.	Unsure/ NA	0	1	2	3	4

	Unsure/ Not Applicable	Never	Rarely	Sometimes	Often	Very Often
6. My spouse and I fight about our children.	Unsure/ NA	0	1	2	3	4
7. I (or my spouse) treat my children negatively or give them less attention during or after our marital conflict.	Unsure/ NA	0	1	2	3	4
8. My children are aware that my spouse and I are considering a divorce.	Unsure/ NA	0	1	2	3	4
9. My children see my spouse and I express affection or support for each other.	Unsure/ NA	4	3	2	1	0
10. My children see my spouse and I resolving conflict in positive ways.	Unsure/ NA	4	3	2	1	0

Now add up your score for these 10 questions: ____
Higher scores indicate that your children are more likely to be aware of a lot of conflict between you and your spouse, while lower scores indicate that your children are less likely to be aware of conflict between you and your spouse. There is no specific score that indicates this, but if your score is **greater than 25,** then your children, if they are old enough, probably are aware of your marital conflict.

❖ Overall, how do you think your children view your marriage? How aware do you think they are of your marital problems?

_____

_____

_____

_____

_____

B. *Changes.* Children may react more negatively to a divorce if it leads to other changes in their lives. Often a divorce can mean moving, less income, and less time with parents. Consider how your children's lives would change if you divorced. Circle the answer that best describes your situation.

Would my children . . .			
1. Maintain current levels of contact with me?	Yes	No	Unsure
2. Maintain current levels of contact with my spouse?	Yes	No	Unsure
3. Maintain contact with current friends/ neighbors?	Yes	No	Unsure
4. Maintain contact with my extended family?	Yes	No	Unsure
5. Maintain contact with my spouse's extended family?	Yes	No	Unsure
6. Live in their current home?	Yes	No	Unsure
7. Start sharing a bedroom (if children currently have their own bedroooms)?	Yes	No	Unsure
8. Attend a different daycare, school, or church?	Yes	No	Unsure
9. Participate in the same extra-curricular activities?	Yes	No	Unsure

Now, think about the following questions and write down your ideas.

❖ How would a divorce (and the custody arrangement) affect my children's daily schedule during the school year?

_____

_____

_____

❖ How would a divorce (and the custody arrangement) affect my children's daily schedule when not in school?

_____

_____

_____

❖ How would a divorce (and the custody arrangement) affect my children's weekend routines?

_____

_____

_____

_____

❖ How would a divorce (and the custody arrangement) affect my children's activities during vacation time?

_____

_____

_____

_____

❖ How would a divorce (and the custody arrangement) affect how my children celebrate holidays?

_____

_____

_____

_____

❖ So, overall, how would a divorce (and the custody arrangement) affect your children's daily lives?

_____

_____

_____

_____

C. *Emotions.* Every child may have an individual and even unexpected reaction to his or her parents' divorce. But given what you know about your children's emotions, reasoning, and expectations, consider how your children might feel if you were to divorce. (You may need to consider this for each child, if their reactions would be different.) Circle any of the emotions listed below that you think your children might feel:

Angry   Confused   Frustrated   Hopeful   Nervous   Scared

Annoyed   Disappointed   Guilty   Left Out   Relieved   Surprised

Betrayed   Excited   Happy   Lonely   Sad   Worried

❖   What other emotions might your children feel?

_____

_____

_____

_____

❖   Why do you think your children would feel these emotions?

_____

_____

_____

_____

_____

_____

_____

D. *Resilience.* As you learned in this chapter, children who are more flexible or adaptive and who have better social skills generally have an easier time adjusting to divorce. Think about the following questions and write down your ideas:

❖ How flexible or adaptable are your children? Do they deal fairly easily with change and different situations or do those things tend to upset them? Are they usually secure or insecure? (You may need to think about this separately for each child.)

_____

_____

_____

_____

_____

❖ Do your children have good social skills or do they struggle with relationships with other children and adults? Is getting along with others easy for them or hard? Do they fit in when they are in groups or do they struggle in groups? (You may need to think about this separately for each child.)

_____

_____

_____

_____

_____

E. *Your Parenting.* Perhaps the most important element in how well your children might adapt to divorce is the quality of the parenting you provide them during the difficult changes of a divorce. The stresses of divorce and your own emotions can affect your parenting. Of course, maybe you are already feeling greater stress and emotions due to challenges you are facing in your marriage. Still, think about the following questions.

❖ Would you be more or less stressed if you got a divorce? How would stress affect your ability to be a good parent? Do you think you might be harsher in disciplining your children? More lenient or soft? How could you keep stress from making you less effective as a parent? Write your thoughts here:

_____

_____

_____

_____

_____

❖ What aspects of parenting would change if you got a divorce? For instance, are there things your spouse usually does as a parent that you would need to take on? How would a divorce affect the amount of time and attention you give your children? Write down your thoughts here:

_____

_____

_____

_____

_____

❖ How might a divorce affect the way you see and treat your children? For instance, would you need your children to be more mature and independent? Would your children need to take on more responsibilities in the home or be alone in the home more often? Would you need your children to be an emotional support to you? (Sometimes after a divorce, parents go to their children for support or sympathy or even advice. While a little of this is understandable, too much of this can place children in the uncomfortable role of acting like a parent to their parent.) Write down your thoughts here:

_____

_____

_____

_____

_____

❖ Usually, the amount of time parents can care directly for their children decreases after a divorce. A divorce often requires different circumstances for caring for children, such as daycare, family care, more babysitting, etc. What kind of changes would you anticipate for caring for your children when you are not able to be there? How do you think your children will react to such changes?

_____

_____

_____

_____

❖ Children do better after divorce if their parents can cooperate with each other and hold down their anger. How well do you think you could cooperate and be civil with your spouse if you got a divorce? Would you be able to speak positively about your ex-spouse in front of your children? Would you feel good if your children wanted to spend a lot of time with your ex-spouse and openly expressed love for him or her? Write down your thoughts here:

_____

_____

_____

_____

_____

F. *Putting It Together.* Now that you've considered these different issues—how your children might feel about your current marriage and how aware they may be of your marital problems, how your children's daily lives might change because of divorce, the emotions your children might feel if you divorce, the personal characteristics of your children that may affect how well they adjust to a divorce, and how a divorce might affect your parenting—how well do you think your children would adjust to a divorce? Write your thoughts here:

_____

_____

_____

_____

_____

_____

_____

_____

[1] Wallerstein, J. S., Lewis, J. M., & Blakeslee, S. (2000). *The unexpected legacy of divorce: A 25 year landmark study.* New York: Hyperion (see p. xxvii).

[2] California Marriage Baseline Survey Findings. (2008). Retrieved from www.camarriage.com

[3] Emery, R. E. (2004). *The truth about children and divorce.* New York: Viking.

[4] Emery, R. E. (2004). *The truth about children and divorce,* New York: Viking.

[5] Amato, P. R., & Booth, A. (1997). *A generation at risk.* Cambridge, MA: Harvard University; Hetherington, E. M., & Kelly, J. (2002). *For better or worse: Divorce reconsidered.* New York: W. W. Norton.

[6] Morrison, D. R., & Coiro, M. J. (1999). Parental conflict and marital disruption: Do children benefit when high-conflict marriages are dissolved? *Journal of Marriage and the Family, 61,* 626–637.

[7] Hetherington, E. M., & Kelly, J. (2002). *For better or worse: Divorce reconsidered.* New York: W. W. Norton (see p. 112).

[8] Hetherington, E. M., & Kelly, J. (2002). *For better or worse: Divorce reconsidered.* New York: W. W. Norton.

[9] Fackrell, T. A., Hawkins, A. J., & Kay, N. M. (2011). How effective are court-affiliated divorcing parents education programs? A meta-analytic study. *Family Court Review, 49,* 107–119; Frieman, B. B., Garon, H. M., & Garon, R. J. (2000). Parenting seminars for divorcing parents: One year later. *Journal of Divorce and Remarriage, 33*(3/4), 129–143; Haine, R. A., Sandler, I. N., Wolchik, S. A., Tein, J., & Dawson-McClure, S. R. (2003). Changing the legacy of divorce: Evidence from prevention programs and future directions. *Family Relations, 52,* 397–405.

[10] Cummings, E. M., & Davies, P. T. (2002). Effects of marital conflict on children: Recent advances and emerging themes in process-oriented research. *Journal of Child Psychology and Psychiatry, 43,* 31–63.

[11] Sturge-Apple, M. L., Davies, P. T., & Cummings, E. M. (2006). Hostility and withdrawal in marital conflict: Effects on parental emotional unavailability and inconsistent discipline. *Journal of Family Psychology, 20,* 227–238. Katz, L., & Gottman, J. (1997). Buffering children from marital conflict and dissolution. *Journal of Clinical Child Psychology, 26,* 157–171.

[12] Kanoy, K., Ulku-Steiner, B., Cox, M., & Burchinal, M. (2003). Marital relationship and individual psychological characteristics that predict physical punishment of children. *Journal of Family Psychology, 17,* 20–28; Katz, L. & Gottman, J. (1997). Buffering children from marital conflict and dissolution. *Journal of Clinical Child Psychology, 26,* 157–171; Sturge-Apple, M. L., Davies, P. T., & Cummings, E. M. (2006). Hostility and withdrawal in marital conflict: Effects on parental emotional unavailability and inconsistent discipline. *Journal of Family Psychology, 20,* 227–238.

[13] Harold, G. T., & Conger, R. D. (1997). Marital conflict and adolescent distress: The role of adolescent awareness. *Child Development, 68,* 333–356.

[14] Doyle, A. B., & Markiewicz, D. (2005). Parenting, marital conflict and adjustment from early- to mid-adolescence: Mediated by adolescent attachment style? *Journal of Youth and Adolescence, 34*, 97–110; Harold, G. T., & Conger, R. D. (1997). Marital conflict and adolescent distress: The role of adolescent awareness. *Child Development, 68*, 333–356; Rubin, K. H., Bukowski, W., & Parker, J. G. (2006). Peer interactions, relationships, and groups. In W. Damon and R. M. Lerner (Series Eds.) & N. Eisenberg (Vol. Ed.), *Handbook of Child Psychology: Vol. 3, Social, Emotional, and Personality Development*. New York: Wiley; Stocker, C. M., Richmond, M. K., Low, S. M., Alexander, E. K., & Elias, N. M. (2003). Marital conflict and children's adjustment: Parental hostility and children's interpretations as mediators. *Social Development, 12*, 149–161.

[15] Kaczynski, K. J., Lindahl, K. M., & Malik, N. M. (2006). Marital conflict, maternal and paternal parenting, and child adjustment: A test of mediation and moderation. *Journal of Family Psychology, 20*, 199–208; Katz, L., & Gottman, J. (1997). Buffering children from marital conflict and dissolution. *Journal of Clinical Child Psychology, 26*, 157–171; Wickrama, K. A. S., Lorenz, F., & Conger, R. (1997). Parental support and adolescent physical health status: A latent growth-curve analysis. *Journal of Health and Social Behavior, 38*, 149–163.

[16] Amato, P. R., & Booth, A. (1996). A prospective study of divorce and parent–child relationships. *Journal of Marriage and the Family, 58*, 356–366.

[17] Amato, P. R., & Booth, A. (1996). A prospective study of divorce and parent–child relationships. *Journal of Marriage and the Family, 58*, 356–366. Grych, J. H., Harold, G. T., & Miles, C. J. (2003). A prospective investigation of appraisals as mediators of the link between interparental conflict and child adjustment. *Child Development, 74*, 1176–1193.

[18] Katz, L., & Gottman, J. (1997). Buffering children from marital conflict and dissolution. *Journal of Clinical Child Psychology, 26*, 157–171.

[19] Katz, L., & Gottman, J. (1997). Buffering children from marital conflict and dissolution. *Journal of Clinical Child Psychology, 26*, 157–171.

[20] Wallerstein, J. S., Lewis, J. M., & Blakeslee, S. (2000). *The unexpected legacy of divorce: A 25 year landmark study*. New York: Hyperion.

[21] Wallerstein, J. S., Lewis, J. M., & Blakeslee, S. (2000). *The unexpected legacy of divorce: A 25 year landmark study*. New York: Hyperion.

[22] Amato, P. R. (2005). The impact of family formation change on the cognitive, social, and emotional well-being of the next generation. *Future of Children, 15*(2), 75–96.

[23] Wallerstein, J. S., Lewis, J. M., & Blakeslee, S. (2000). *The unexpected legacy of divorce: A 25 year landmark study*. New York: Hyperion.

[24] Waite, L. J., & Gallagher, M. (2000). *The case for marriage*. New York: Doubleday.

[25] Wallerstein, J. S., Lewis, J. M., & Blakeslee, S. (2000). *The unexpected legacy of divorce: A 25 year landmark study*. New York: Hyperion.

[26] Wallerstein, J. S., Lewis, J. M., & Blakeslee, S. (2000). *The unexpected legacy of divorce: A 25 year landmark study.* New York: Hyperion.

[27] Wallerstein, J. S., Lewis, J. M., & Blakeslee, S. (2000). *The unexpected legacy of divorce: A 25 year landmark study.* New York: Hyperion.

[28] Amato, P. R., & Keith, B. (1991). Parental divorce and the well-being of children: A meta-analysis. *Psychological Bulletin, 110,* 26–46.

[29] Wallerstein, J., & Lewis, J. (2004). The unexpected legacy of divorce. *Psychoanalytic Psychology, 21,* 353–370.

[30] Barber, B., & Eccles, J. (1992). Long-term influence of divorce and single parenting on adolescent family- and work-related values, behaviors, and aspirations. *Psychological Bulletin, 111,* 108–126; Zill, N., Morrison, D., & Coiro, M. (1993). Long-term effects of parental divorce on parent–child relationships, adjustment, and achievement in young adulthood. *Journal of Family Psychology, 7,* 91–103.

[31] Amato, P. R., & Keith, B. (1991). Parental divorce and the well-being of children: A meta-analysis. *Psychological Bulletin, 110,* 26–46.

[32] Amato, P. R. (2001). Children of divorce in the 1990s: An update of the Amato and Keith (1991) meta-analysis. *Journal of Family Psychology, 15,* 355–370.

[33] Amato, P. R. (2005). The impact of family formation change on the cognitive, social, and emotional well-being of the next generation. *Future of Children, 15*(2), 75–96; Emery, R. E. (2004). *The truth about children and divorce.* New York: Viking; Hetherington, E. M., & Kelly, J. (2002). *For better or worse: Divorce reconsidered.* New York: W. W. Norton.

[34] Zill, N., Morrison, D., & Coiro, M. (1993). Long-term effects of parental divorce on parent–child relationships, adjustment, and achievement in young adulthood. *Journal of Family Psychology, 7,* 91–103.

[35] Amato, P. R. (2000). The consequences of divorce for adults and children. *Journal of Marriage and the Family, 62,* 1269–1287.

[36] Barber, B., & Eccles, J. (1992). Long-term influence of divorce and single parenting on adolescent family- and work-related values, behaviors, and aspirations. *Psychological Bulletin, 111,* 108–126; Hetherington, E. M., & Kelly, J. (2002). *For better or worse: Divorce reconsidered.* New York: W. W. Norton.

[37] Dawson, D. (1991). Family structure and children's health and well-being: Data from the 1988 National Health Interview Survey on Child Health. *Journal of Marriage and the Family, 53,* 573–584.

[38] Dawson, D. (1991). Family structure and children's health and well-being: Data from the 1988 National Health Interview Survey on Child Health. *Journal of Marriage and the Family, 53,* 573–584.

[39] Angel, R., & Worobey, J. L. (1988). Single motherhood and children's health. *Journal of Health and Social Behavior, 29,* 38–52.

[40] Waite, L. J., & Gallagher, M. (2000). *The case for marriage.* New York: Doubleday.

[41] Amato, P., & Keith, K. (1991). Parental divorce and the well-being of children: A meta-analysis. *Psychological Bulletin, 110*, 26–46.

[42] Aro, H., & Palosaari, U. (1992). Parental divorce, adolescence, and transition to young adulthood: A follow-up study. *American Journal of Orthopsychiatry, 62*, 421–429.

[43] Wallerstein, J., & Lewis, J. (2004). The unexpected legacy of divorce. *Psychoanalytic Psychology, 21*, 353–370.

[44] Amato, P., & Keith, K. (1991). Parental divorce and the well-being of children: A meta-analysis. *Psychological Bulletin, 110*, 26–46.

[45] Amato, P., & Keith, K. (1991). Parental divorce and the well-being of children: A meta-analysis. *Psychological Bulletin, 110*, 26–46.

[46] Wallerstein, J. S., Lewis, J. M., & Blakeslee, S. (2000). *The unexpected legacy of divorce: A 25 year landmark study.* New York: Hyperion.

[47] Tucker, J., & Friedman, H. (1997). Parental divorce: Effects on individual behavior and longevity. *Journal of Personality and Social Psychology, 73*, 381–391; Wallerstein, J. S., Lewis, J. M., & Blakeslee, S. (2000). *The unexpected legacy of divorce: A 25 year landmark study.* New York: Hyperion.

[48] Marquardt, E. (2005). *Between two worlds: The inner lives of children of divorce.* New York: Crown (see p. 208). In addition, for a recent overview of research in this area, see Marquardt, E., Ziettlow, A., & Stokes, C. E. (2013). *Does the shape of families shape faith?* New York: Institute for American Values.

[49] Marquardt, E. (2005). *Between two worlds: The inner lives of children of divorce.* New York: Crown (see pp. 212–214).

[50] Marquardt, E. (2005). *Between two worlds: The inner lives of children of divorce.* New York: Crown (see pp. 207, 210).

[51] Marquardt, E. (2005). *Between two worlds: The inner lives of children of divorce.* New York: Crown (see p. 147).

[52] Marquardt, E. (2005). *Between two worlds: The inner lives of children of divorce.* New York: Crown (see p. 143).

[53] Marquardt, E. (2005). *Between two worlds: The inner lives of children of divorce.* New York: Crown (see p. 150).

[54] Woodward, L., Fergusson, D. M., & Horwood, L. J. (2001). Risk factors and life processes associated with teenage pregnancy: Results of a prospective study from birth to 20 years. *Journal of Marriage and the Family, 63*, 1170–1184; Wu, L. L., & Martinson, B. C. (1993). Family structure and the risk of a premarital birth. *American Sociological Review, 58*, 210–232.

[55] Longmore, M. A., Manning, W. D., & Giordano, P. C. (2001). Preadolescent parenting strategies and teens' dating and sexual initiation: A longitudinal analysis. *Journal of Marriage and Family, 63*, 322–335.

[56] Amato, P. R. (2005). The impact of family formation change on the cognitive, social, and emotional well-being of the next generation. *Future of Children, 15*(2), 75–96; Davis, E. C., & Friel, L. V. (2001). Adolescent sexuality:

Disentangling the effects of family structure and family context. *Journal of Marriage and Family, 63*, 669–681.

[57] Oman, R. F., Vesely, S. V., & Aspy, C. B. (2005). Youth assets and sexual risk behavior: The importance of assets for youth residing in one-parent households. *Perspectives on Sexual and Reproductive Health, 37*(1), 26; Woodward, L., Fergusson, D. M., & Horwood, L. J. (2001). Risk factors and life processes associated with teenage pregnancy: Results of a prospective study from birth to 20 years. *Journal of Marriage and Family, 63*, 1170–1184.

[58] Amato, P. R., & DeBoer, D. D. (2001). The transmission of marital instability across generations: Relationship skills or commitment to marriage? *Journal of Marriage and Family, 63*, 1038–1051; Wolfinger, N. (2005). *Understanding the divorce cycle: The children of divorce in their own marriages.* New York: Cambridge University.

[59] Amato, P. R., & DeBoer, D. D. (2001). The transmission of marital instability across generations: Relationship skills or commitment to marriage? *Journal of Marriage and Family, 63*, 1038–1051.

[60] Shulman, S., Scharf, M., & Lumer, D. (2001). Parental divorce and young adult children's romantic relationships: Resolution of the divorce experience. *American Journal of Orthopsychiatry, 71*, 473–478; Wallerstein, J. S., Lewis, J. M., & Blakeslee, S. (2000). *The unexpected legacy of divorce: A 25 year landmark study.* New York: Hyperion.

[61] Dush, C. M. K., Cohan, C. L., & Amato, P. R. (2003). The relationship between cohabitation and marital quality and stability: Change across cohorts? *Journal of Marriage and Family, 65*, 539–549; Jose, A., O'Leary, D., & Moyer, A. (2010). Does premarital cohabitation predict subsequent marital stability and marital quality? A meta-analysis. *Journal of Marriage and Family, 72*, 105–116; Teachman, J. (2003). Premarital sex, premarital cohabitation, and the risk of subsequent marital dissolution among women. *Journal of Marriage and Family, 65*, 444–455.

[62] Rhoades, G. K., Stanley, S. M., & Markman, H. J. (2009a). The pre-engagement cohabitation effect: A replication and extension of previous findings. *Journal of Family Psychology, 23*, 107–111; Rhoades, G. K., Stanley, S. M., & Markman, H. J. (2009b). Working with cohabitation in relationship education and therapy. *Journal of Couple & Relationship Therapy, 8*, 95–112.

What Are the Possible Consequences of Divorce for Adults?

[I]ndividuals who make the decision to divorce need to be well-informed about its potential costs to themselves, their partners, and their children. When spouses are preoccupied with their own immediate frustrations and disappointment, family experts have a responsibility to remind them of the long-term investment they have in each other and in their children.

—Drs. Linda J. Waite & Maggie Gallagher, noted marriage researchers[1]

Overview: Compared to adults in a stable marriage, divorced adults, on average, have poorer physical and mental health. They experience more social isolation. After a few years, most divorced fathers do not have regular contact with their children. For some divorced adults, new romantic relationships help rebuild self-esteem and happiness, but for others, new romantic relationships end up producing greater feelings of loneliness, unhappiness, and lower self-esteem. Many individuals struggle to manage their emotional ties to their ex-spouse. They continue to be dependent on them for emotional support and practical matters. They remain deeply attached even though the legal ties have been broken. Continuing strong attachment to the ex-spouse makes it harder for adults to adjust to divorce. There are a number of factors that help individuals adjust better to divorce, such as the ability to embrace change.

Parents at the crossroads of divorce have many questions about the possible effects of divorce on their children. But they also have questions about how a divorce might affect them. This chapter examines the research evidence on the effects of divorce on adults. We save a discussion of the financial effects of divorce for the next chapter.

A. Why do some adults thrive and others struggle after divorce?

Nearly all people enter marriage with the hope and expectation that their marriage will be a lifelong, mutually rewarding relationship. So it's not surprising that divorce is a painful experience for almost everyone.[2] Some newly divorced individuals experience temporary setbacks but end up adjusting well while others find themselves on a downward slope that almost never seems to end.[3] Some people are better able to handle the stresses and challenges and new opportunities of divorce than others. Researchers have found a number of factors that help us understand why some people seem to do better than others after divorce.

Breaking Away from High-Conflict Marriages. Individuals who are ending a marriage with chronic high conflict or violence, on average, are happier over time.[4] Escaping the stress of a high-conflict relationship and the personal threat to safety, not surprisingly, can lead to a better situation, even with the other challenges that often accompany divorce. (Exercise 2.5, "How Healthy Is My Marriage?" at the end of Chapter 2 may help you assess the level of conflict in your relationship [especially items 22–30 in the relationship quiz], along with other aspects of your relationship. Exercise 4.4, "Is There Abuse in My Marriage?" at the end of Chapter 4 may help you assess whether there is violence in your relationship.)

Embracing Change. As hard as it can be sometimes, embracing the opportunity for change helps many people deal better with divorce. The most successful divorced individuals are men and women who embrace the opportunity to make changes in their lives. They work on maintaining friendships or establishing new ones. They embrace employment opportunities and often return to school; they explore and test the options and avenues available to them.[5] Perhaps this helps explain why people with more education adjust easier after divorce; they are better able to solve their problems and they feel more in control of their lives during this difficult transition time.[6] Some women report that the early years of divorce are a time of significant personal growth; they thrive on the increased independence and personal choices.[7] Those who can feel good about the possibilities for change after a divorce don't just talk about making a better life; they work and sacrifice to make life better. This attitude and effort then begins to open up new opportunities and relationships.[8] Each time a divorced person makes a choice—about how to earn a living, about where to live, about what kind of daycare center or school to send children to, or about when to start dating—he or she is making a choice about whether or not to embrace the chance for positive change following a divorce. Each choice leads to another choice and these choices begin to fold into one another until they form a pattern and the individual is on the road to making life better.[9] Research has found that individuals tend to adjust better to divorce if they have more personal resources, such as higher income or education level.[10] It is possible that having resources such as these give individuals more positive opportunities, making it easier to embrace the change associated with divorce.

On the other hand, many struggle to take those first steps toward positive change in the early years following divorce. It's easy for newly divorced individuals, particularly those with fewer resources, to be preoccupied with the immediate stresses of life following divorce. When just getting through today's problems seems overwhelming, it's hard to do big-picture thinking and embrace long-term change. Worn down by day-to-day efforts just to get by, some divorced people become overwhelmed by the stresses they are experiencing. Some can sink into a sense of failure, purposelessness, or depression, causing some to turn to drugs or alcohol for a release from the stress. For some, divorce can set in motion a process in which they end up losing everything—jobs, homes, children, and self-esteem. Fortunately, studies have found that most of these problems—unhappiness, depression, alcohol abuse, etc.— have largely subsided two to three years after the divorce.[11] But this does not necessarily mean that divorced adults have rebuilt happy lives after a few years. Even when they eventually manage to rebuild a functional new life, some find little joy and satisfaction in that new life.[12]

Attitude Toward the Divorce. Of course, it's easier to embrace change when you wanted the marriage to end and have an accepting attitude toward divorce.[13] In most cases, however, one of the spouses does not want the divorce.[14] When someone is still committed to the marriage and views the divorce as a personal tragedy, then he or she tends to have a more difficult time after divorce.[15] So, unfortunately, often the person who didn't want the divorce usually has a harder time adjusting to post-divorce life than the person who initiated it. Those who still have positive feelings toward their ex-spouses tend to feel more distress as the result of divorce.[16] Individuals in this situation may benefit from staying involved with others socially and developing a new romantic relationship.[17] However, holding negative feelings toward an ex-spouse can make it harder to adjust to a divorce. Individuals may have an easier time adjusting to a divorce if they avoid conflict during divorce so that they experience less negative emotion toward their ex-spouses.[18]

Insecurity and Attachment to the Ex-Spouse. As we mentioned in Chapter 4, insecure individuals—those who are emotionally dependent on their spouses and/or have a fear of abandonment—may also find it harder to adjust to divorce. Research has found that insecure individuals are typically willing to stay in a marriage even if they are not satisfied with the marriage.[19] Understandably, these insecure individuals tend to have a harder time adjusting to life after divorce; secure individuals tend to adjust to divorce better. First, they report only mild, rather than high, distress as a result of their divorce, and they see it as less threatening.[20] These individuals also view themselves as being more capable of coping with divorce, and in fact, research does show that they use more effective problem-solving strategies, such as better negotiating and reasoning skills.[21] As a result, these individuals experience fewer physical and psychological health problems after divorce.[22] They also report feeling more comfortable with themselves and others and experiencing fewer problems with their former spouse.[23] In addition, these individuals also generally use more positive parenting skills after divorce,[24] which may help their children better adjust to life after divorce.

It's hard to know how divorce will affect you personally. It's hard to know if you are one of those who can embrace change with divorce or if you will be worn down by it. You may benefit from doing the Exercise 6.1, "How Will Divorce Affect Me Personally?" at the end of this chapter. It will help you think about these issues and your personal circumstances.

B. What are the possible emotional and physical health consequences of divorce?

For some, leaving a very difficult marriage is a path—albeit a difficult one—to building a better, happier life. However, as we discussed earlier in Chapter 3, for many others, divorce trades one set of challenges for another. Overall, researchers have found that, compared to adults in a stable marriage, divorced adults have poorer physical and mental health, other things being equal.[25] In our interview with Janet, who had been divorced for more than 15 years, she described herself as an emotional and physical wreck as a result of her divorce: "I weighed like 50 pounds less than I do now; … stress makes me lose weight. Everyone would always ask me if I had an eating disorder, I was so thin."

Of course, researchers have also found some positive benefits to divorce for some individuals, and we will review those findings too. But the overall picture documents how hard the process of family breakdown can be on adults, not just children. Below is a partial list of some of the physical and emotional problems that are more common among divorced individuals compared to married individuals.

❖ *Happiness.* Divorced adults are generally less happy.[26]

❖ *Depression.* Divorced individuals, particularly women, are more vulnerable to depression. They have higher levels of psychological stress, lower levels of general psychological well-being, and poorer self-esteem.[27]

❖ *Health.* Divorced individuals see a doctor more often and are more likely to suffer from serious illnesses.[28] Some of these health problems diminish over time. But individuals who experience a divorce are more likely to die at earlier ages.[29]

❖ *Alcohol/Drugs.* Divorced adults drink more alcohol than married adults and account for the highest proportion of heavy drinkers. This is especially true for men.[30] This isn't too surprising given that research shows that men and women—but especially men— generally reduce their use of drugs and alcohol when they marry.[31]

Although divorced individuals do go through a period of stress, many bounce back after a few years. Some individuals will bounce back quicker given certain circumstances, such as divorcing at younger ages, higher income and education, and higher levels of social support from family and friends.[32]

C. What are the possible consequences of divorce for social support?

The decision to divorce can bring about major changes in the social lives of individuals. Compared to married individuals, divorced individuals are less involved in social activities[33] and report more social isolation.[34] Being involved socially is often difficult because accomplishing the day-to-day activities of home, work, and childcare is often more difficult to do alone.[35] Divorced adults often face greater loneliness than married individuals. In addition to losing a spouse, they also lose many of their social contacts such as in-laws, married friends, and neighbors.[36] The loss of these social contacts often results in the loss of emotional support.

Divorced individuals often find that friends disappear following the divorce. Often friends, even close friends, distance themselves from the divorced individual because they do not know what to say or do to make the person feel better or they are not interested in continually talking about the divorce and the changes associated with it. Although the newly divorced individual desires to maintain friendships and be involved socially, many complain they feel socially awkward because they struggle with whether or not they still fit into social activities as a single person.

Also, divorced individuals find they have less in common with their married friends. Many times friends sort themselves into "his" friends and "her" friends. And married friends may see the newly divorced person as a possible threat to the stability of their own marriages.[37] Married friends often find it difficult to sustain independent friendships with both sides of a divided couple because the newly divorced person is often wrapped up with the struggles and challenges of single life.[38]

The amount of social activity that men and women experience varies, because divorced men and women generally approach the transition into single life differently. Divorced men report a more lasting attachment to their ex-spouses than divorced women.[39] Often, to compensate for losing their spouse, male social activities tend to rise rapidly and dramatically following divorce.[40] Many divorced women seek out a support group to help in their single-life adjustment.[41] Friends help the newly divorced woman get a new perspective on the divorce.[42] Women like to talk about their problems while men are more likely to "tough it out" than "talk it out."[43] Men often have fewer close friends to rely on for support after divorce. In addition to men losing their spouses, they are at greater risk of losing contact with their children as well.

One such man we know, devastated by divorce, began to drink heavily and use other addictive drugs. This problem, when discovered, resulted in legal changes to his co-parenting arrangement. He ended up having to pay for supervised visitation with his children until he became more stable. This was financially costly for both spouses because they had to use the court to deal with the substance abuse and control the conflict after their divorce.

Following a divorce, children usually reside with only one parent, most often the mother.[44] This increases the amount of loneliness men feel after divorce. Most fathers make real efforts to stay involved with their children even if they do not have custody and live together. But research indicates that after a few years, most divorced fathers do not have regular contact with their children.[45] The ex-wife and children of one father we know moved across the country after the divorce. His visitation is limited by the expense of the airline tickets to transport his children back and forth for visitation. Therefore, he can only afford about two visits a year, which makes it difficult to have a solid relationship with his growing and developing children. When a friend of his was considering a divorce, this divorced father encouraged him to think seriously and try as hard as possible to make the marriage work.

And it's not just the quantity of father–child contact that suffers; it is common for the quality of these relationships to deteriorate, as well.[46] The proportion of single fathers raising their children has tripled in the past generation.[47] However, having custody of the children often creates more social isolation because fathers must deal with the challenges of being a single parent.[48] Men as well as women find it difficult to be successful at work and home and still find time for a social life.

Even though parents love their children and want to be with them, the children often add an emotional strain on both mothers and fathers. Single parents struggle with trying to balance being a parent and being involved socially. The balancing act between being a parent and having a social life can have a negative effect on the parents' happiness.[49] Both men and women who have custody of their children face more isolation because they are less active in social activities and have fewer friends than married individuals.[50] Many divorced mothers report that meeting the needs of their children limits them from being socially active.[51]

One single mother we know admitted how difficult it is to parent full time with little or no breaks. When visitation comes for the children's father, she is happy to be able to spend a little time on herself. Still, her work schedule and the back and forth on the weekends associated with her children's visitation with their father limits her ability to socialize.

Although work can be a source of stress for mothers during a divorce transition, it can also be a source of social support. Newly divorced working women generally feel less depressed and less isolated than divorced stay-at-home mothers.[52] Working mothers have adult company that can help them to feel better about themselves as they work to rebuild their lives.

D. What are the possible consequences of divorce for religious involvement?

For many people who have strong ties to a personal faith or religious group, marriage often plays a central part in their personal worship. For them, marriage is not just a vow with their spouse, but also a covenant made with God. Because couples can feel like God is a part of their union, approving it and sanctifying it, when these marriages dissolve, feelings of spiritual failure, guilt, and a broken relationship with God sometimes arise.[53] This is even stronger when individuals feel responsible for the breakup of a marital union.[54] Divorcing individuals may therefore feel cut off from a dimension of their life that gave them access to sacred, spiritual feelings and support. Some will even go so far as to feel that they deserve to be cut off from God or their religious friends, feeling that they were not as good or loving or forgiving or patient as they should have been.[55] This kind of sacred loss is linked to higher rates of depression.[56]

When one spouse feels that the other has purposefully violated sacred covenants, their marriage, which was once regarded as sacred, may now seem desecrated—something which was precious to them is now "dirty" or defiled—and this leads to even greater anger compared to other kinds of loss.[57] Sometimes, those with strong religious convictions may feel that their spouse could have violated such a sacred thing only if he or she were under the influence of evil forces or not living according to God's expectations. This outlook can cause a parent to guard the children from the ex-spouse, and has potential for long-lasting conflict after the divorce is over.

In many cases, adults (and children) end up leaving or switching their religious group as a consequence of divorce.[58] Some may feel embarrassment or resentment; others may feel that they are spiritual failures or outcasts. They may feel that they either deserve to be cut off or are not worthy to participate in worship services. Many families move to different neighborhoods or cities with a divorce, which may necessitate switching familiar congregations. But for many, religious beliefs and activities can be a powerful support to help families deal with the challenges they are facing. Counseling with trusted religious leaders and accepting their support during these difficult times can be very helpful.

E. What are the possible consequences of divorce for romantic relationships?

Most who divorce hope to find a more satisfying relationship in the future. Exploring new romantic relationships after divorce can be both exciting and stressful. One important study that followed divorcing individuals for many years after their divorces found that a new romantic relationship after divorce often produced an increase in self-esteem, a decline in feelings of depression, and even decreased health complaints and visits to the doctor.[59] These positive outcomes were found when the new relationships provided a sense of security and support and when there was real concern for each other. However, this study also found that some divorced women and men (especially) used casual sex to find the closeness and intimacy that they were missing. These researchers observed that casual sex frequently ended up producing greater feelings of loneliness, unhappiness, and lower self-esteem. Moreover, these feelings sometimes led to substance abuse, which made problems worse. So new romantic relationships after divorce are a bit of a two-edged sword: healthy, caring relationships can be helpful, but relationships based on casual sex can make things worse. When dating again, it makes sense to be cautious and go slowly.

In addition, we heard from several of the people we interviewed that moving on to another romantic relationship wasn't easy. Laura divorced her unfaithful husband but struggled to move on:

> So yeah, do you move on? You try. Does it get any easier? No. And it doesn't matter who comes in your life. I have a great boyfriend right now. ... But [my marriage] was 12 long years. It's going to take a long time to get [past] that.

For Janet, trying to find a new love had left her exhausted:

> I have really not dated [in a long-term relationship] since [the divorce]. Because ... when I finally extracted myself from that, I realized that, even though the circumstances were so different than my marriage, there were a lot of similarities. And as they say, the common denominator in all your failed relationships is you. ... I was exhausted from trying to make things work with people that it ultimately wasn't going to work with. ... And I sort of liken it to a love slot machine; you keep putting in hoping that it will pay out and you spend all of your time sitting in front of the slot machine and feeding it.

F. What are the possible consequences of divorce for your relationship with your ex-spouse?

It's often easier to end a relationship legally than it is to end it emotionally. A court will divide up property and specify other responsibilities, such as child support. But a court cannot decree a clean emotional break. Despite divorce, many have a continuing emotional attachment to their ex-spouses.[60] This was clear in our interviews with those who had experienced a divorce. Researchers have found two kinds of continuing attachment. One is a continuing preoccupation with and/or dependence on the ex-spouse. A second kind of emotional attachment is ongoing hostility towards the ex-spouse. Researchers have found that continuing emotional attachment to an ex-spouse is associated with a variety of psychological problems, including depression, anxiety, loneliness, anger, and feelings of powerlessness.[61]

Not surprisingly, hostile emotional attachments have the most negative effects. Researchers have found that the more hostile the divorce process and the higher the level of conflict after the divorce, the harder it is for individuals to adjust in healthy ways and move on with their lives. This also makes it harder on the children.[62] Researchers have found that some couples seem unable to let go of their hostility and conflict even a decade later.[63] It's helpful for both adults and children when ex-spouses try hard to hold down natural feelings of anger during the divorce and let those feelings go after the divorce. Of course, this is easier said than done. In these cases, personal counseling to deal with the emotional transitions associated with the divorce can be very helpful.

One such couple we know were married in their teenage years. But they soon divorced. Their struggles to co-parent their children after divorce escalated as each thought the other was being unreasonable. The mother resented any visitation with the father and the father fought in court often to enforce his visitation. They rarely spoke to one another and used their attorney and the court to communicate and make decisions for their family.

What may be surprising to some is that many individuals struggle to cut their more positive emotional ties to their ex-spouse. They continue to be dependent on them for emotional support and practical matters. They remain deeply attached even though the legal ties have been broken. Researchers have found continuing strong attachment to the ex-spouse makes it harder for adults to adjust to divorce and can contribute to psychological problems.[64] Laura, as you just read, was struggling to move on because of how emotionally attached she was to her ex-spouse:

> It's been two years since my divorce and you can see that we still have a major connection, and it's terrible. It's terrible to feel that way. Because even now we talk, "What the heck have we done?" … It's still really, really hard. I really, really did and still do, deeply, deeply love him. … Even now, it's just been a nightmare because we're still so connected. …You've told this person everything in life. He knows everything about you. … He's called me about a bazillion times to tell me how unhappy he is. In the 3 years since the separation and the 2 years since the divorce, the longest that we have gone without speaking to each other has been one week. … I don't think there's another man on the earth that I

care for as much as I do for him. But people don't understand that, they don't understand those feelings. …
And this is coming from a girl that was cheated on; he got another woman pregnant, and he really, really betrayed me.

To show how complex divorce can be, one study found that sometimes maintaining a good relationship with the ex-spouse and working together to be good parents to the children went hand-in-hand with continuing emotional attachment to the ex-spouse, which makes personal adjustment to divorce harder.[65] There is a fine line between maintaining a positive, working relationship with your ex-spouse and remaining emotionally dependent on him or her. Healthy post-divorce relationships have clearly established boundaries that define the former spouse as a co-parent you work with for the good of your children but not as a person you continue to rely on for emotional support.[66]

Exercises for Chapter 6

6.1: How Will Divorce Affect Me Personally?

It may be impossible to know for sure how you will be affected by divorce. But there are many things to think about that will give you a better sense of what may happen. Below are a series of questions about different aspects of your life after a divorce.

A. *Your Social Life.* In this chapter, you learned that many people report having a difficult time maintaining friendships and feeling lonely after divorce. This exercise is designed to help you think how a divorce may affect your social life. (A later part of this exercise will focus specifically on romantic relationships after divorce. For now, think about friendships and family relationships.)

Friends. Who are your strongest friends and how might those friendships be affected by a divorce? (Next you will focus on relationships with family members.) Write down your thoughts about this:

Name of Friend	How might your relationship be affected by a divorce? Why?

Family. Of course, family relationships are often the most important part of our social lives. Now consider how divorce may affect your social relationships with various family members. Include relationships with, for instance, parents, siblings, extended family, and in-laws. Of course, especially consider how divorce may affect your relationship with your children. (Next you will focus on your relationship with your ex-spouse.) Write down your thoughts about this:

Name of Family Member	How might your relationship be affected by a divorce? Why?

Ex-Spouse. Now think about how your divorce will affect your relationship with your ex-spouse. For some, conflict decreases after divorce but for others it increases. Some can cut the emotional and practical ties fairly easily but others remain quite attached and dependent on the ex-spouse. Think about how this is likely to be for you. Write your thoughts here:

_____

_____

_____

_____

_____

_____

_____

_____

Future Romance. Of course, most people who divorce hope to find a new and better love. What are your hopes and dreams? What barriers will you face to realizing these hopes? Be as realistic, honest, and specific as possible in assessing this. How can you meet and overcome these barriers? Write your thoughts here:

_____

_____

_____

_____

_____

_____

_____

_____

_____

_____

_____

_____

B. *Your Religious Life.* In this chapter, you also learned about the effects that divorce may have on your religious life. You may not have thought much about this aspect of your life after divorce. This exercise is designed to help you do so.

Beliefs. What are your religious beliefs about divorce? How will they affect how you adjust to divorce? Will they be a source of strength to you or might they make adjustment harder? Why? Write down your thoughts here:

_____

_____

_____

_____

_____

_____

_____

Support. Do you think you will have support and help from religious leaders and friends? Or do you think you might feel alienated from religious support as a result of your divorce? Why? Write down your thoughts here:

_____

_____

_____

_____

_____

Activity. Will you want to maintain your involvement with your religious group? Increase it? Decrease it? Why? What challenges will you face with respect to religious involvement after your divorce? Write down your thoughts here:

_____

_____

_____

_____

_____

_____

C. *Change.* In this chapter you learned that those who can embrace the big changes that come with divorce and optimistically work to make their lives better, not surprisingly, are able to adjust better to divorce. Try to assess your personality and attitudes about change. First, rate yourself with the following questions.[67] Circle the answers that best describe you.

How much or how often do these words or phrases describe you?					
	Never	Rarely	Some-times	Often	Very Often
A. Open-minded	0	1	2	3	4
B. Flexible	0	1	2	3	4
C. Easygoing	0	1	2	3	4
D. Adaptable	0	1	2	3	4

Now add up your score (it should be between 0–16): _____
* ❖ Higher scores indicate that you are more adaptable and flexible person.
* ❖ If your score is **less than 10,** then adaptability and flexibility are probably not strengths of yours. You may struggle more than others to adjust to the significant changes brought on by divorce.
* ❖ If your score is **10 or higher,** then adaptability and flexibility are probably strengths of yours. Although this doesn't mean that you will have an easy time adjusting to a divorce, your ability to adapt to change may help you adjust better to the significant changes brought on by divorce.

Having completed this brief scale, now think about the following questions, answering them as honestly as possible:

Flexibility. Are you a person who can adjust fairly easily to changes or is that hard for you? Are you pretty flexible or pretty set in your ways? Write down your thoughts here:

_____

_____

_____

_____

Attitude. What is your attitude about the changes that would need to come for you to adjust to divorce? Do you think you will embrace them or get worn down by them? Do you think you have the energy to pursue needed changes or will you struggle just to get by day to day? Would you welcome a divorce or would you dread it? Write down your thoughts here:

_____

_____

_____

_____

_____

_____

_____

D. *Putting It All Together.* So, having thought about how divorce might affect your social and religious life and whether you would embrace change or struggle with it, what does it all mean for you? How well do you think you would adjust to divorce? Or do you think it would be better for you to keep trying to repair your marriage and avoid divorce, if you could? Write down your final thoughts here:

_____

_____

_____

_____

_____

[1] Waite, L. J., & Gallagher, M. (2000). *The case for marriage.* New York: Doubleday (see p. 189).

[2] Amato, P. R. (2000). The consequences of divorce for adults and children. *Journal of Marriage and Family, 62*, 1269–1287.

[3] Amato, P. R. (2000). The consequences of divorce for adults and children. *Journal of Marriage and Family, 62*, 1269–1287.

[4] Amato, P. R., & Hohmann-Marriott, B. (2007). A comparison of high- and low-distress marriages that end in divorce. *Journal of Marriage and Family, 69*, 621–638.

[5] Hetherington, E. M., & Kelly, J. (2002). *For better or for worse: Divorce reconsidered.* New York: W. W. Norton.

[6] Wang, H., & Amato, P. R. (2000). Predictors of divorce adjustment: Stressors, resources, and definitions. *Journal of Marriage and Family, 62*, 655–668.

[7] Amato, P. R. (2000). The consequences of divorce for adults and children. *Journal of Marriage and the Family, 62*, 1269–1287.

[8] Hetherington, E. M., & Kelly, J. (2002). *For better or for worse: Divorce reconsidered.* New York: W. W. Norton.

[9] Hetherington, E. M., & Kelly, J. (2002). *For better or for worse: Divorce reconsidered.* New York: W. W. Norton.

[10] Tschann, J. M., Johnston, J. R., & Wallerstein, J. S. (1989). Resources, stressors, and attachment as predictors of adult adjustment after divorce: A longitudinal study. *Journal of Marriage and the Family, 51*, 1033–1046.

[11] Amato, P. R. (2000). The consequences of divorce for adults and children. *Journal of Marriage and the Family, 62*, 1269–1287.

[12] Hetherington, E. M., & Kelly, J. (2002). *For better or for worse: Divorce reconsidered.* New York: W. W. Norton.

[13] Amato, P. R. (2000). The consequences of divorce for adults and children. *Journal of Marriage and Family, 62*, 1269–1287.

[14] Waite, L., Browning, D., Doherty, W., Gallagher, M., Luo, Y., & Stanley, S. (2002). *Does divorce make people happy? Findings from a study of unhappy marriages.* New York: Institute for American Values.

[15] Amato, P. R. (2000). The consequences of divorce for adults and children. *Journal of Marriage and Family, 62*, 1269–1287.

[16] Berman, W. H. (1988). The role of attachment in the post-divorce experience. *Journal of Personality and Social Psychology, 54*, 9–503.

[17] Tschann, J. M., Johnston, J. R., & Wallerstein, J. S. (1989). Resources, stressors, and attachment as predictors of adult adjustment after divorce: A longitudinal study. *Journal of Marriage and the Family, 51*, 1033–1046.

[18] Tschann, J. M., Johnston, J. R., & Wallerstein, J. S. (1989). Resources, stressors, and attachment as predictors of adult adjustment after divorce: A longitudinal study. *Journal of Marriage and the Family, 51*, 1033–1046.

[19] Davila, J., & Bradbury, T. N. (2001). Attachment insecurity and the distinction between unhappy spouses who do and do not divorce. *Journal of Family Psychology, 15*, 371–393.

[20] Birnbaum, G. E., Orr, I., Milkulincer, M., & Florian, V. (1997). When marriage breaks up—Does attachment style contribute to coping and mental health? *Journal of Social and Personal Relationships, 14*, 643–654.

[21] Birnbaum, G. E., Orr, I., Milkulincer, M., & Florian, V. (1997). When marriage breaks up—Does attachment style contribute to coping and mental health? *Journal of Social and Personal Relationships, 14*, 643–654.

[22] Birnbaum, G. E., Orr, I., Milkulincer, M., & Florian, V. (1997). When marriage breaks up—Does attachment style contribute to coping and mental health? *Journal of Social and Personal Relationships, 14*, 643–654; Cary, H. H. (2000). Attachment status and post-divorce adjustment. *Dissertation Abstracts International, 61*(8-B), 4445. (UMI 9964950).

[23] Clipper, R. C. (1997). Adult attachment models and their relationship to adjustment to divorce. *Dissertation Abstracts International, 58*(1-A), 0094. (UMI 9718125).

[24] Vareschi, C. G., & Bursik, K. (2005). Attachment style differences in the parental interactions and adaptation patterns of divorcing parents. *Journal of Divorce and Remarriage, 42*, 15–32.

[25] Aseltine, R. H., Jr., & Kessler, R. C. (1993). Marital disruption and depression in a community sample. *Journal of Health and Social Behavior, 34*, 237–251.

[26] Aseltine, R. H., Jr., & Kessler, R. C. (1993). Marital disruption and depression in a community sample. *Journal of Health and Social Behavior, 34*, 237–251; Amato, P. R. (2000). The consequences of divorce for adults and children. *Journal of Marriage and the Family, 62*, 1269–1287.

[27] Aseltine, R. H. Jr., & Kessler, R. C. (1993). Marital disruption and depression in a community sample. *Journal of Health and Social Behavior, 34*, 237–251; Amato, P. R. (2000). The consequences of divorce for adults and children. *Journal of Marriage and the Family, 62*, 1269–1287.

[28] Amato, P. R. (2000). The consequences of divorce for adults and children. *Journal of Marriage and the Family, 62*, 1269–1287; Booth, A., & Amato, P. (1991). Divorce and psychological stress. *Journal of Health and Social Behavior, 32*, 396–407.

[29] Lillard, L. A., & Waite, L. J. (1995). 'Til death do us part: Marital disruption and mortality. *American Journal of Sociology, 100*, 1131–1156.

[30] Calahan, D., Cisin, J. H., & Crossley, H. M. (1969). *American drinking practices.* New Haven, CT: College and University Press; Umberson, D., & Willliams, C. L. (1993). Divorced fathers: Parental role strain and psychological distress. *Journal of Family Issues, 14*, 378–400.

[31] Duncan, G. J., Wilkerson, B., & England, P. (2006). Cleaning up their act: The effects of marriage and cohabitation on licit and illicit drug use. *Demography, 43*, 691–710.

[32] Booth, A., & Amato, P. (1991). Divorce and psychological stress. *Journal of Health and Social Behavior, 32*, 396–407.

[33] Hetherington, E. M., & Kelly, J. (2002). *For better or for worse: Divorce reconsidered.* New York: W. W. Norton.

[34] Amato, P. R. (2002). The consequences of divorce for adults and children. *Journal of Marriage and Family, 62,* 1269–1287.

[35] Hetherington, E. M., & Kelly, J. (2002). *For better or for worse: Divorce reconsidered.* New York: W. W. Norton & Company.

[36] Amato, P. R. (2002). The consequences of divorce for adults and children. *Journal of Marriage and Family, 62,* 1269–1287.

[37] Kitson, G. C., & Morgan, L. A. (1990). The multiple consequences of divorce: A decade review. *Journal of Marriage and the Family, 54,* 913–924.

[38] Hetherington, E. M., & Kelly, J. (2002). *For better or for worse: Divorce reconsidered.* New York: W. W. Norton.

[39] Wang, H., & Amato, P. R. (2000). Predictors of divorce adjustment: Stressors, resources, and definitions. *Journal of Marriage and Family, 62,* 655–668.

[40] Hetherington, E. M., & Kelly, J. (2002). *For better or for worse: Divorce reconsidered.* New York: W. W. Norton.

[41] Hetherington, E. M., & Kelly, J. (2002). *For better or for worse: Divorce reconsidered.* New York: W. W. Norton.

[42] Hetherington, E. M., & Kelly, J. (2002). *For better or for worse: Divorce reconsidered.* New York: W. W. Norton.

[43] Hetherington, E. M., & Kelly, J. (2002). *For better or for worse: Divorce reconsidered.* New York: W. W. Norton.

[44] Kitson, G. C., & Morgan, L. A. (1990). The multiple consequences of divorce: A decade review. *Journal of Marriage and the Family, 54,* 913–924.

[45] Cabrera, N., Shannon, J. D., Vogel, C., Tamis-LeMonda, C., Ryan, R. M., Brooks-Gunn, J., Raikes, H., Cohen, R. (2004). Low-income fathers' involvement in their toddlers' lives: Biological fathers from the Early Head Start Research and Evaluation study. *Fathering, 2,* 5–30; Stewart, S. D. (2003). Nonresident parenting and adolescent adjustment: The quality of nonresident father–child interaction. *Journal of Family Issues, 24,* 217–244.

[46] Amato, P. R., & Booth, A. (1996). A prospective study of divorce and parent–child relationships. *Journal of Marriage and the Family, 58,* 356–365.

[47] Grief, G. L. (1995). Single fathers with custody following separation and divorce. *Marriage & Family Review, 20*(1/2), 213–231.

[48] Wang, H., & Amato, P. R. (2000). Predictors of divorce adjustment: stressors, resources, and definitions. *Journal of Marriage and Family, 62,* 655–668.

[49] Wang, H., & Amato, P. R. (2000). Predictors of divorce adjustment: stressors, resources, and definitions. *Journal of Marriage and Family, 62,* 655–668.

[50] Wang, H., & Amato, P. R. (2000). Predictors of divorce adjustment: stressors, resources, and definitions. *Journal of Marriage and Family, 62,* 655–668.

[51] Hetherington, E. M., & Kelly, J. (2002). *For better or for worse: Divorce reconsidered.* New York: W. W. Norton.

[52] Hetherington, E. M., & Kelly, J. (2002). *For better or for worse: Divorce reconsidered.* New York: W. W. Norton.

[53] Livingston, P. H. (1985) Union and disunion. *Studies in Spirituality, 6*, 241–253.

[54] Mahoney, A., Pargament, K. I., Murray-Swank, A., & Murray-Swank, N. (2003). Religion and sanctification of family relationships. *Review of Religious Research, 44*, 220–236.

[55] Livingston, P. H. (1985) Union and disunion. *Studies in Spirituality, 6*, 241–253.

[56] Mahoney, A., & Tarakeshwar, N. (2005). Religion's hold in marriage and parenting in daily life and during family crisis. In R. F. Paloutzian & C. L. Park (Eds.) *Handbook of the psychology of religion and spirituality* (pp. 177–195). New York: Guildford.

[57] Mahoney, A., & Tarakeshwar, N. (2005). Religion's hold in marriage and parenting in daily life and during family crisis. In R. F. Paloutzian & C. L. Park (Eds.) *Handbook of the psychology of religion and spirituality* (pp. 177–195). New York: Guildford.

[58] Freigelman, W., Gormand, B. S., & Varacalli, J. A. (1992). Americans who give up religion. *Sociology and Social Research, 76*, 138–143; Lawton, L. E., & Bures, R. (2001). Parental divorce and "switching" religious identity. *Journal for the Scientific Study of Religion, 40*, 99–111.

[59] Hetherington, E. M., & Kelly, J. (2002). *For better or for worse: Divorce reconsidered.* New York: W. W. Norton.

[60] Emery, R. E. (1994). *Renegotiating family relationships: Divorce, child custody, and mediation.* New York: Guilford.

[61] Madden-Derdich, D. A., & Arditti, J. A. (1999). The ties that bind: Attachment between former spouses. *Family Relations, 48*, 244-249.

[62] Madden-Derdich, D. A., & Arditti, J. A. (1999). The ties that bind: Attachment between former spouses. *Family Relations, 48*, 244–249.

[63] Sbarra, D. A., & Emery, R. E. (2005). Coparenting conflict, nonacceptance, and depression among divorced adults: Results from a 12-year follow-up study of child custody mediation using multiple imputation. *American Journal of Orthopsychiatry, 75*, 63–75.

[64] Emery, R. E. (1994). *Renegotiating family relationships: Divorce, child custody, and mediation.* New York: Guilford; Kitson, G. C. (1992). *Portrait of divorce: Adjustment to marital breakdown.* New York: Guildford.

[65] Madden-Derdich, D. A., & Arditti, J. A. (1999). The ties that bind: Attachment between former spouses. *Family Relations, 48*, 244-249.

[66] Madden-Derdich, D. A., & Arditti, J. A. (1999). The ties that bind: Attachment between former spouses. *Family Relations, 48*, 244–249.

[67] These questions are taken from the RELATE Relationship Questionnaire and are used with permission. See Busby, D. M., Holman, T. B., & Taniguchi, N. (2001). RELATE: Relationship evaluation of the individual, family, cultural, and couple contexts. *Family Relations, 50*, 308–316.

Chapter 7

What Are the Possible
Financial Consequences of Divorce?

When it comes to building wealth or avoiding poverty, a
stable marriage may be your most important asset.

Drs. Linda J. Waite & Maggie Gallagher,
noted marriage researchers[1]

Overview: Divorce is financially stressful. Researchers estimate
that divorcing individuals would need more than a 30% increase
in income, on average, to maintain the same standard of living
they had prior to their divorce. About one in five women fall into
poverty as a result of divorce. Three out of four divorced
mothers don't receive full payment of child support. Most men
experience a loss in their standard of living in the years after a
divorce, as well, a loss generally about 10%–40%, depending on
circumstances. Divorce also impacts communities. One national
study estimated the cost of family breakdown in the United
States at more than $100 billion a year.

Previous chapters have dealt with the social and psychological
impacts of divorce for children and adults. This chapter focuses on the
financial impact of divorce. Understandably, this is a worry for most
people at the crossroads of divorce. In our interview, Janet described the
financial dilemma she faced at the crossroads of her eventual divorce:

[My husband] made good money and we had a house, and so
the alternative to being there with this person who disliked
me was being with two little kids on my own, trying to make
it, or being in a comfortable home with a person who made a
decent income and who loved my children.

Financial challenges as a result of divorce are common. The process
of divorce is expensive. The income that used to support one household
is split and now must support two households. All possessions, money,
financial assets, and debt acquired during (and sometimes before)
marriage are divided between former spouses. Researchers estimate that
divorcing individuals would need more than a 30% increase in income,

on average, to maintain the same standard of living they had prior to their divorce.[2] So divorce is financially stressful, especially for poorer couples. On the other hand, researchers have learned that a stable marriage is one of the best paths to building and maintaining wealth.[3] We also know that women, men, and children experience the financial consequences of divorce somewhat differently.

A. What are the possible financial consequences of divorce for women and children?

Most children—five out of six—live with their mothers after a divorce, so the financial effects of divorce on women and children are largely the same.[4] Generally, women suffer more from financial losses than men because of unequal wages for men and women and because women usually have more expenses associated with the physical custody of children after divorce.[5] Research has found:

❖ About one in five women fall into poverty as a result of divorce.[6]

❖ About one in three women who own a home and have children at home when they divorce lose their homes.[7]

❖ Three out of four divorced mothers don't receive full payment of child support.[8]

The financial burden is greatest during the first year after divorce and varies for each woman depending on how much money she contributed to the family income before divorce and the ability and willingness of her former husband to make support payments. If she was already earning a decent income and her husband can be relied on to make full child-support payments, then the financial stress of divorce will not be as great. But many women are not prepared financially for life as a single parent. As a result, a significant number often need to rely on public assistance (welfare) programs to supplement their family finances. This financial support is crucial for many women, although it is still unlikely to cover all financial needs. Women at the crossroads of divorce should evaluate their financial situation carefully. Good preparation for the financial challenges of divorce is important to minimize its negative effects. You may benefit from some thinking, planning, and calculations based on the activities and questions in Exercise 7.1, "Thinking About the Financial Consequences of Divorce," at the end of this chapter.

One woman we know struggled after divorce when she realized it would be impossible for her to stay home with her children, which is something she really valued and enjoyed. The financial consequences of divorce showed her that it was very expensive to run two households for a family. She was not granted alimony payments to support her desire to be at home full time with her children. For children, the financial burdens of divorce may affect their lives in a number of ways. A parent who may have previously been able to stay at home with children or work only part time often will find it necessary to work full time after the parents separate. Children may receive less attention and care from their parents as a result. Fathers paying child support may feel that they are doing all that is necessary or possible for their children financially. When combined with the mother's usually lower income, that may mean the children will not be able to experience many opportunities, such as music lessons or summer activities, that their friends may participate in. Furthermore, public schools have begun to charge fees for participation in extracurricular activities such as sports, choir, or drama, and divorced parents may not be able to pay for these "extras." This not only deprives children of potentially valuable experiences but distinguishes them from their more affluent friends and leaves them without ways to constructively spend after-school time. Finally, standard child support payments almost always end when a child turns 18—just at the point where the child needs additional financial help in order to continue his or her education in college or a vocational program. Children may feel that the noncustodial parent does not care for them because of these lost opportunities—they may be aware of the custodial parent's financial struggles, but unaware of the financial situation of the noncustodial parent.

Although parents can negotiate higher child support than is mandated by a state's child support schedule, can require that an employed parent or parent with better employment benefits keep the children on a health insurance plan, and can negotiate help with school and other fees and even with support for college, these agreements can be ignored by the responsible parent—although he or she may have entered them in good faith. The other parent must return to court in order to enforce these agreements, as well as any unpaid child-support owed, which is expensive and time-consuming. Also, emergencies or expenses related to the children's health that are not covered by insurance, for example a chronic illness or orthodontic care, may have been unforeseen at the time of divorce and will require further financial negotiation between the parents. Finally, if the noncustodial parent remarries and has additional children, the competing demands of that parent's new children with those of the children of the previous marriage may result in perceived and actual inequities between the children of the two families. These inequities may affect support of and opportunities for the older children as well as their relationship with the noncustodial parent.

Even with careful preparation for the financial impact of divorce, money problems are common. Research suggests that women usually don't recover fully from the financial consequences of divorce until they remarry.[9] Alimony payments are uncommon these days, but if a spouse does receive them, they stop when the paying spouse dies or the receiving spouse remarries.

B. What are the possible financial consequences of divorce for men?

Some people seem to believe that men are financially better off after a divorce than they were during their marriage. Good research shows that this is a myth. Because most families now have two incomes, most men experience a loss in their standard of living in the years after a divorce, a loss generally between 10%–40%, depending on circumstances.[10] Two factors contribute to this financial loss. First, if his ex-wife contributed a substantial income to the family, he will struggle to make up for this lost second income. Second, he is likely to be required to make child-support and other payments.[11] This comes on top of having to pay for a separate home or apartment. In addition, if a father has custody or shares custody of his children, there will be additional expenses.

Similar to women, how much men lose financially from divorce varies depending on the amount of money he contributed to the family's income. Men who provided less than 80% of a family's income before divorce suffer more financially from divorce. This is the case for most men nowadays. Men who provided more than 80% of a family's income before a divorce do not suffer as much financial loss, and may even improve their financial situation somewhat.[12]

One man we know who was divorced three times was underemployed and felt the financial burden of paying child support to all three families. Most of his paycheck was garnished (taken directly from his check before it got to him) by the state's Office of Recovery Services. He could barely live on the remaining amount and was angry that he had no control over how much child support he could pay since the amount is determined by a preset formula that does not take into account his special circumstances.

You may benefit from doing Exercise 7.1, "Thinking About the Financial Consequences of Divorce," at the end of the chapter, to get a better idea of how divorce would affect you. Of course, if you are able to repair your marriage rather than divorce, you will likely be better off financially in both the short and long term.

C. What is the financial impact of divorce on communities and taxpayers?

Women and men at the crossroads of divorce have a lot of financial issues to think about. It's understandable that they are focused on their personal financial concerns. But divorce is more than a personal issue; it is also a very public issue. Divorce is one of the most common ways that people, especially women and children, fall into poverty.[13] When people fall into poverty, they usually take advantage of government programs, services, and supports, paid for with taxes. In addition, children from divorced homes are more likely to get involved in deviant behavior and crime, which cost governments a great deal of taxpayer money.[14] Also, there are more long-term, hard-to-quantify financial impacts on society. Children from divorced homes struggle more in school and are less likely to be able to go to college.[15] Our economy depends more and more on a well-educated workforce. And of course, personal incomes increase with education.

Although it is hard to get a solid estimate of the costs of divorce to taxpayers, one nationwide study conservatively estimated the cost each year of divorce and unwed childbearing at $112 billion.[16] A Texas study estimated the cost in that state each year to be more than $3 billion.[17] It is important to note that these costs are just for the welfare-related claims that could be made by families that experience divorce; they don't take into consideration the actual costs of the divorce itself (e.g., lawyer and court fees, counseling, mediation, etc.).

Divorce is sometimes necessary. A free and just society recognizes this necessity and compassionately provides some financial help to those negatively affected by divorce. But we should also recognize that society takes on a heavy financial burden when marriages fail. Marriage and divorce are public issues as well as private concerns.[18] The success and failure of our marriages have consequences beyond our personal lives. Individuals at the crossroads of divorce help not just themselves and their families but their neighborhoods, communities, and nation when they are able to repair their relationships and establish a healthy, stable marriage.

7.1: Thinking About the Financial Consequences of Divorce

Dividing the family finances when a couple divorces can be much more complicated and stressful than people often realize, even if you and your spouse can be cooperative and civil. It takes a lot of time and detailed work to separate your financial lives. This exercise encourages you to detail your family finances and think more about what effect divorce will have.

A. *Employment Details*. List employment details for yourself and your spouse.

Your Employer:	Your Job Title:
Your Gross Annual Income:	Your Gross Monthly Income:
Your Net Monthly Income:	Your Other Income (pensions, rents, child support, second job, etc.):
Spouse's Employer:	Spouse's Job Title:
Spouse's Gross Annual Income:	Spouse's Gross Monthly Income:
Spouse's Net Monthly Income:	Spouse's Other Income (pensions, rents, child support, second job, etc.):

B. *Financial Assets*. List property and automobiles and fill in the information requested.

Real Property (homes, land, etc.):
Property #1 (list):
Address:
Date of Purchase:
Purchase Price:
Down Payment:
Source of Down Payment:

Owing Balance on First Mortgage:
Owing Balance on Second Mortgage:
Current Appraisal Value:
Monthly Payment:
Title Held By:
Equity:
Lot Description (Must have this for legal paperwork.):
Property #2 (list):
Address:
Date of Purchase:
Purchase Price:
Down Payment:
Source of Down Payment:
Owing Balance on First Mortgage:
Owing Balance on Second Mortgage:
Current Appraisal Value:
Monthly Payment:
Title Held By:
Equity:
Lot Description (Must have this for legal paperwork.):
Do you or your spouse have property that either of you will inherit? Value?
Do you have timeshare property? Value?
Automobiles, Recreational Vehicles, etc.
Vehicle #1
Year:
Model and Make:
Title Held By:
Balance Owed:
Monthly Payment:
Current Bluebook Value:
Equity:
Present Possession:
Vehicle #2
Year:
Model and Make:
Title Held By:

Balance Owed:
Monthly Payment:
Current Bluebook Value:
Equity:
Present Possession:
Vehicle #3
Year:
Model and Make:
Title Held By:
Balance Owed:
Monthly Payment:
Current Bluebook Value:
Equity:
Present Possession:

C. *Personal Property.* List your valuable personal property items (e.g., jewelry, computer), their financial worth, and any money you may owe on that item.

Personal Property	
Item: Worth: Balance Owing:	Item: Worth: Balance Owing:
Item: Worth: Balance Owing:	Item: Worth: Balance Owing:
Item: Worth: Balance Owing:	Item: Worth: Balance Owing:
Item: Worth: Balance Owing:	Item: Worth: Balance Owing:
Item: Worth: Balance Owing:	Item: Worth: Balance Owing:
Item: Worth: Balance Owing:	Item: Worth: Balance Owing:

D. *Financial Accounts*. List your (and your spouse's) joint and separate financial accounts, including checking, savings, retirement, stocks, etc.

Checking Account Amount:	Savings Account Amount:
Pension #1 Worth:	Pension #2 Worth:
401K #1 Worth:	401K #2 Worth:
Stock 1: Current Value:	Stock 2: Current Value:
Cemetery Plots:	
Life Insurance Plan #1 Premium: Beneficiary: Amount:	Life Insurance Plan #2 Premium: Beneficiary: Amount:
Are you expecting a federal or state income tax return this year? In what amount or amounts?	
IRA #1: Amount:	IRA #2: Amount:

E. *Business Interests*. List any business interests you and your spouse have and their value.

Business Interest #1:	Value:
Business Interest #2:	Value:

F. *Debts and Obligations*. List current debts and other financial obligations you and your spouse have and record the information requested about them. Include estimated federal or state income tax you may owe this year.

Name of Debt:	Purpose:	Balance Owing:	Monthly Payment:	In Whose Name:

G. *Anticipated Monthly Expenses After Divorce.* Do some financial planning about how you will meet your monthly financial expenses if you divorce. Estimate the amount for each expense (if it applies to your situation). Then add up the expenses. Finally, try to estimate your anticipated monthly income. Then compare your expenses to your income.

Monthly Expenses	Estimated $	Comments
Mortgage/Rent		
Property Tax		
House/Rental Insurance		
Food/Household Supplies		
Utilities		
Clothing		
Uninsured Medical Expenses		
Uninsured Dental Expenses		
Childcare		
Health Insurance Premiums		
Education Expenses		
Automobile Loan Payment		
Automobile Gas, Maintenance, Insurance		
Donations to Church and other Charities		
Entertainment Funds		
Misc. for Children:		
Other: Retirement Savings (401k, employer		

pension plan, IRA)		
Other:		
Other:		
Total Expenses:		
Monthly Income		
Employment		
Interest Income		
Support Payments from Spouse		
Other income:		
Other income:		
Total Income:		
Difference (Income - Expenses or Expenses - Income):		

H. *Thinking Ahead Financially.* It has probably taken a lot of time and effort to fill out the information in the forms above. But if you have done this, you are in a better position to answer the following questions that are important to consider when you are considering divorce. Review some of your calculations above and try your best to answer honestly the following questions.[19] Some of the questions may not be applicable to your situation.

1. Do you have adequate money saved that would help support you and your children after the divorce, especially in the first few years when money can be extra tight?

    _____

    _____

2. Do you have home furnishings, a car, and other possessions you will need after the divorce, or will you need to purchase them?

    _____

    _____

3. Have you paid off your debt as much as possible? How much debt will be assigned to you after the divorce?

    _____

4. Who will count the children as withholding exemptions for income tax purposes? Often, the parent who pays child support claims this right, but since child support is never enough to cover the overhead (home, utilities, car repairs, miscellaneous expenses) or pay half the expenses of rearing children, the custodial parent should insist on claiming this benefit.

5. Also for federal (and some state) tax purposes, the custodial parent should claim the Earned Income Tax Credit (EITC) for heads of household with dependents. See the instructions to Form 1040 about dependents, withholding exemptions, support as it relates to custody arrangements, and the EITC.

6. Do you have adequate education or training necessary to provide for your children and yourself after the divorce? If not, how will you get that education or training?

7. Will you need and can you afford childcare if you have to go to work full time after the divorce?

8. Will your work provide healthcare benefits for yourself and your children? Will your spouse's work cover health benefits for your children if they don't live with him/her?

9. Does your work provide pension/retirement plans or can you invest for retirement as an individual? In order to receive half the value of your ex-spouse's retirement accounts (based on the years when you were married) at the time of his or her retirement, you must provide a

form called a QUADRO (Qualified Domestic Relations Order) to the administrator of each of your ex-spouse's retirement accounts at the time of the divorce. You will need an experienced lawyer's help with this.

_____

_____

10. If you don't have all the things you will need to provide for yourself and your children after the divorce, how long will it take you to get them, and how will you get them?

_____

_____

11. Is it possible that you and your ex-spouse could set up college savings funds for your children, so they will not be disadvantaged by the divorce but still receive help with college? If possible, try to make this payment a part of the final divorce decree, separate from child support payments.

_____

_____

12. It is difficult to maintain your financial lifestyle after divorce. What are some things that you could give up to save money?

_____

_____

13. There are many other smaller family expenses that we sometimes forget about, such as lessons for piano, ballet, karate, etc., extra-curricular school activity fees (e.g., sports, choir, etc.), summer camp, scouting, and many more. How would you cover these kinds of expenses that are important for your children?

_____

_____

_____

H. *What Does All This Mean?* Now, having considered all these things, what do you think about the possible financial consequences of a divorce? Are you optimistic that you can make things work? Are you concerned? Why? Write down your thoughts and feelings:

_____

_____

_____

_____

_____

_____

_____

_____

Endnotes to Chapter 7

[1] Waite, L. J., & Gallagher, M. (2000). *The case for marriage.* New York: Doubleday (see p. 123).

[2] Sayer, L. C. (2006). Economic aspects of divorce and relationship dissolution. In M. A. Fine & J. Harvey (Eds.), *Handbook of divorce and relationship dissolution* (pp. 385–406). Mahwah, NJ: Lawrence Erlbaum.

[3] Waite, L. J., & Gallagher, M. (2000). *The case for marriage.* New York: Doubleday.

[4] Grall, T. S. (2001). *Custodial mothers and fathers and their child support: 2001* (Current Population Reports, Series P60-225). Washington, DC: U.S. Government Printing Office.

[5] Sayer, L. C. (2006). Economic aspects of divorce and relationship dissolution. In M. A. Fine & J. Harvey (Eds.), *Handbook of divorce and relationship dissolution* (pp. 385–406). Mahwah, NJ: Lawrence Erlbaum.

[6] Grall, T. S. (2003) *Custodial mothers and fathers and their child support: 2003* (Current Population Reports, Series P60-230). Washington, DC: U.S. Government Printing Office.

[7] Hanson, T. L., McLanahan, S., & Thomson, E. (1998). Windows on divorce: Before and after. *Social Science Research, 27*, 329–349.

[8] Grall, T. S. (2003) *Custodial mothers and fathers and their child support: 2003* (Current Population Reports, Series P60-230). Washington, DC: U.S. Government Printing Office.

[9] Smock, P. J., Manning, W. D., & Gupta, S. (1999). The effect of marriage and divorce on women's economic well-being. *American Sociological Review, 64*, 794–812.

[10] Sayer, L. C. (2006). Economic aspects of divorce and relationship dissolution. In M. A. Fine & J. Harvey (Eds.), *Handbook of divorce and relationship dissolution* (pp. 385–406). Mahwah, NJ: Lawrence Erlbaum.

[11] McManus, P. A., & DiPrete, T. A. (2001). Losers and winners: The financial consequences of separation and divorce for men. *American Sociological Review, 66*, 246–268.

[12] McManus, P. A., & DiPrete, T. A. (2001). Losers and winners: The financial consequences of separation and divorce for men. *American Sociological Review, 66*, 246–268.

[13] Bianchi, S. (1999). The gender gap in the economic well being of nonresident fathers and custodial mothers. *Demography, 36*, 195–203; Smock, P. J., Manning, W. D., & Gupta, S. (1999). The effect of marriage and divorce on women's economic well-being. *American Sociological Review, 64*, 794–812.

[14] Institute for Marriage and Public Policy. (2005). *Can married parents prevent crime? Recent research on family structure and delinquency 2000–2005.* Washington DC: Institute for Marriage and Public Policy; Institute for American Values. (2005). *Why marriage matters: Twenty-six conclusions from the social sciences.* New York: Author.

[15] Amato, P. R. (2000). The consequences of divorce for adults and children. *Journal of Marriage and the Family, 62*, 1279–1287; Furstenberg, F. F., & Kiernan, K. E. (2001). Delayed parental divorce: How much do children benefit? *Journal of Marriage and Family, 63*, 452; White, L., & Rogers, S. J. (2000). Economic circumstances and family outcomes: A review of the 1990s. *Journal of Marriage and the Family, 62*, 1035–1051.

[16] Scafidi, B. (2008). *The taxpayer costs of divorce and unwed childbearing*: *First-ever estimates for the nation and all fifty states.* New York: Institute for American Values.

[17] Schramm, D. G., Harris, S. M., Whiting, J. B., Hawkins, A. J., Brown, M., & Porter, R. (2013). Economic costs and policy implications associated with divorce: Texas as a case study. *Journal of Divorce and Remarriage, 54*, 1–24.

[18] Nock, S. L. (2005). Marriage as a public issue. *Future of Children, 15*(2), 13–32.

[19] These questions were suggested in Fowlke, L. D. (2004). *Thinking divorce? Think again.* Orem, UT: Fowlken Press (see pp. 30–33).

What Are the Legal Options for Divorce? What Should I Expect During the Divorce Process?

Do not file for divorce in haste. Explore all options and make a conscientious decision, contemplating the short-term and long-term consequences. Once a decision to divorce has been made, remember the law of integrity. What you put into the divorce will surely be what comes out of the divorce. Aggression is normally combated with aggression and compromise is normally embraced with compromise. In the beginning of the separation, although difficult, invest the time and energy to build cooperative patterns for a long-term benefit for you and your children.

Tamara Fackrell, domestic attorney & mediator

Overview. Divorce law varies from state to state in the United States. The divorce process can take anywhere from one month to several years. Some states have a waiting period for the divorce to be completed. Most people use lawyers when going through the divorce process. The divorce process can be expensive. There are some services available to help low-income individuals with their divorces, especially if there has been abuse in the marriage. For straightforward and "uncontested" divorces, some states offer an online court assistance program, with online legal forms needed for divorce that individuals can fill out themselves. Many people choose mediation as an option for divorce. Mediation is a process where a trained, neutral professional will try to help couples reach agreements about issues related to their divorce. Divorcing spouses can still use their lawyers during the mediation process. Mediation is usually less expensive and faster than litigation. Some divorcing couples use "collaborative law," in which they use lawyers who agree to work cooperatively to resolve issues surrounding divorce rather than in an adversarial manner. One spouse may not want the divorce, but it is probably futile to try and challenge the divorce in court because of the way our laws are written and interpreted by the courts.

If a divorce is on the horizon for you, whether you want it or not, it is best to understand the legal process that you are about to experience. And there are some legal choices you need to make. This chapter will help you understand what lies ahead.

A. What should I expect going through the negotiated divorce process?

For most people, the legal process of divorce is an emotionally and financially draining process. When children are involved, parents need to try to be their best selves for the benefit of the children, despite the stresses and challenges.

Divorce laws vary from state to state. This is a general overview of the law. You will probably need to look up specific information for your state.

Many states have a waiting period for divorce.[1] Some states require a waiting period of separation before the legal process begins. Other states have a waiting period after filing a Petition (or Complaint) for Divorce. About half of states have no waiting period requirement. For those states that do have a waiting requirement, 30 days is the most common waiting period to finalize a divorce. But some states have 60-, 90-, or 180-day waiting periods. Louisiana has a 1-year waiting period for divorcing parents. For some states, waiting periods may be longer if you have dependent children. (For a list of requirements for your state, we recommend that you consult the American Bar Association website: http://www.americanbar.org/groups/family_law/resources/family_law_in _the_50_states.html)

Also, if a couple has children, many state laws require them to attend a divorcing parents class for parents before the divorce can be finalized.[2] If the couple does not have children, these courses are not required.

Some couples may decide to reconcile after they have filed the divorce. The divorce process is not final until the Decree of Divorce has been filed with the court, signed by a judge, and filed with the county clerk. Anytime before the divorce decree is filed, a couple can reconcile and their marriage is still legal and binding. Other couples choose an alternate route to divorce and have a time of separation. Separation can be done formally through the court or can be done more informally with agreement between the spouses. For informal separations, agreements made on financial obligations, support, and visitation are best done in writing and signed by both parties. Some parties choose to involve the Office of Recovery Services (ORS), Division of Child Support (DCS), or a similar state agency to help with their case for child support even when they have decided just to separate and not divorce. These are agencies that help parents to collect their child support monies. There is usually a small fee attached to the monthly collection. If a separated couple wants to use the ORS or DCS, most states will require a legal separation, declaration of paternity, or order of the court

The divorce process can take anywhere from 30 days to several years, depending on how many issues can be resolved between spouses. Issues to be settled in divorce are commonly parenting time, division of financial assets and debts, child support, and alimony.[3] And within each of these issues there are many things to be considered. You may benefit from doing exercise 8.1, "Thinking About Parenting Time With Children," at the end of this chapter. Exercise 7.1, "Thinking About the Financial Consequences of Divorce," at the end of Chapter 7, will help you think about all the details associated with dividing your finances. We recommend that you do that exercise. Then, you may benefit from doing Exercise 8.2, "Thinking About Child Support and Alimony," at the end of this chapter.

The logistics of taking one family and dividing it into two households can be difficult. Most of the time, this requires both parents to be employed. Even if a person decides not to work and stay home, the court may "impute"[4] income to that parent for child support calculation. Child support may also deduct medical costs, childcare expenses, and have an offset for additional overnights spent with the other parent.[5] Imputation assigns a potential yearly wage to each parent, even though the parent is not currently working. Most courts also require each spouse to show proof of income through current pay stubs and the previous years' taxes.[6] Attorneys or mediators will also require documentation for all assets and debts in order to gather the legal information needed to divide up all your financial assets.

B. Does getting a divorce require a lawyer or can I get a divorce without the help of a lawyer?

These days, some couples use lawyers to get a divorce and some do not. People who have a lower income *and* who have experienced physical abuse from their spouse sometimes can qualify for a free attorney through the State. Other states have Legal Aid options that are available on the basis of the parties' incomes. But free, long-term legal services are available usually only if there is domestic violence involved in the marriage and if lawyers are available. Low-income individuals also can file paperwork in order to waive the filing fees associated with divorce.[7]

But you do not have to use a lawyer to divorce. Sometimes people choose to act *pro se,* which means people represent themselves in court without a lawyer. This is usually done in simple divorce cases where all matters are agreed upon. If the case has unresolved issues, this can be overwhelming and you will need to do a lot of research in order to file the correct legal pleadings. Further, if your finances involve self-employment businesses or large retirement funds, you may find it very difficult to proceed without a lawyer.

If the divorce is uncontested, which means that both spouses agree on every issue in the divorce, some states have online court programs where people can get access to legal forms and do their own paperwork. State courts usually have a website and forms may be available electronically. If the divorce is contested, mediation can be used to try to resolve the contested issues before or after hiring lawyers. These options are discussed in further detail below.

C. What does it cost to get a divorce?

It is no secret that divorces can be very expensive. Many attorneys require a retainer of several thousand dollars before taking the case. The more spouses disagree, the more expensive the divorce process will cost. If the case goes to litigation in court, the process can cost anywhere from $4,000 to $30,000 dollars per person or even more for each spouse. Courts rarely order one spouse to pay the other spouse's attorney's fees and costs, even if one of the spouses is or was engaged in infidelity, abuse, or other activities that undermined the marriage.

Having an uncontested divorce, where divorcing spouses agree on every item in the divorce, is the least expensive option. Some spouses will choose to have a "kitchen table negotiation" where they work out all of the details of the divorce themselves. Then an attorney can be hired to file "uncontested paperwork," which usually costs between $800 and $2,000 as a total cost.

If a person does file uncontested paperwork, the question arises whether the couple should hire a single attorney or each spouse should hire his or her own attorney. According to the rules of ethics for attorneys, an attorney cannot represent both the divorcing husband and wife.[8] Legally, the attorney is required to represent just one spouse. It is wise for the other spouse to at least get a 1-hour consultation with an attorney to review the uncontested paperwork. Sometimes attorneys will give a free initial consultation. Depending on the facts of the case, a person may not need to get an attorney, but at least having a minimum consultation is a good idea. Another option in these cases is using an Attorney-Mediator. If the mediator you choose is also an attorney, then some state laws allow the Attorney-Mediator to file the divorce paperwork.[9] However, a consultation with an independent attorney is still a good idea.

If the state in which a person resides offers an online option for divorce, this is often an affordable way to file uncontested divorce paperwork. This online system is only meant for those having uncontested issues with simple financial assets and debts, standard child visitation agreements, and court-dictated child support. This system works well for simple divorce cases where few adjustments need to be made. As a caution, however, many people will use the online systems but make substantial changes; they do not phrase the contract language correctly. This may result in future problems that require going back to court, which can be very expensive. If you or your spouse is unwilling or unable to agree on some items, divorce mediation may be a less expensive option to get the divorce issues resolved. (See the next section for more information.)

If you and your spouse cannot or will not agree, many states have statutory provisions that set guidelines for your divorce. Most states have mandated child support guidelines requiring that a certain amount of child support be paid (usually by the noncustodial parent only) based on the number of children and each parent's income. No parents can agree that a parent pay less than the guidelines provided, although they can agree to higher payments. Similarly, detailed visitation guidelines provide for the noncustodial parent to spend time with the children, based on the age of the child and a complicated system that alternates years (even or odd) for how the child divides time between parents on Christmas, the child's birthday, school holidays, etc. Parents may want to take a look at these guidelines, which specify times for pick up and return of the child, before they decide they can't come up with something easier on the child. The court can order supervised visitation (often by a social worker at a place with activities or toys for the child, for a fee) if a parent can be shown to be a potential threat to the child. The court can also order that the child be picked up and dropped off at a neutral site (such as the local police station) if parents fight or express hostility when the child is picked up or dropped off at the child's home. Some states have businesses that specialize in visitation and exchange centers for divorcing parents. Some of these facilities are established through state statute.[10] These businesses can do calendaring, help with parental communication, and facilitate exchanges of the children. High-conflict cases can benefit from using such services. Of course, these business services can be expensive, so not everyone can make use of them.

D. What is divorce mediation? And what are the financial consequences of choosing mediation services for a divorce?

Mediation is legally defined as "a private forum in which one or more impartial persons facilitate communication between parties to a civil action to promote a mutually acceptable resolution or settlement."[11] So, mediation is a process where a neutral person goes through all of the legal issues of the divorce with the divorcing spouses. This neutral person is called a mediator. The mediator is not a decision maker but will try to help the spouses negotiate the terms of their divorce. This includes dividing financial assets and debts, parenting time and custody, alimony, and child support. The mediator can help the divorcing spouses, if they are willing, to settle every issue in the divorce. The mediator will draft a Memorandum of Understanding detailing all of the agreements between the two divorcing spouses. This memorandum can be filed with the court by lodging it with the court or changing it to a stipulation. The filed agreement with the court can be legally enforced.[12] However, divorcing spouses must still file all of their legal paperwork to finalize the divorce.

A mediator can be an attorney, a counselor, or another person specifically trained in mediation.[13] If mediators are attorneys, they will not be acting in their role as attorneys and will not give legal advice to either of the divorcing spouses. However, mediators are skilled in divorce law and this knowledge can be helpful to the process. Some states have a list of approved mediators.

Mediation for a divorce usually takes 2 to 10 hours and is done in one or several sessions, depending on the complexity of the case. The more divorcing parents are able to agree upon, the faster the process will go. So it is a good idea to do a lot of thinking about the issues you will need to settle before you begin meeting with a mediator. You may benefit from doing Exercise 8.3, "Preparing for Divorce Mediation," at the end of this chapter. You may also want to ask the mediator if you will be signing the agreement on the day of mediation. This will prepare you for the process of mediation and the expectations regarding the agreement.

Mediators who deal with family issues usually charge from $100 to

$350 an hour. The cost of divorce mediation therefore generally ranges from about $200 to $3,000 dollars. Traditionally, this cost is divided evenly between the divorcing spouses. Using mediation forums, which require co-mediation, is usually not cost effective because you are paying for two mediators instead of just one. Often people have attorneys and use them for legal counsel during mediation. Some people choose to bring their attorneys to mediation sessions, while others choose to confer (sometimes by telephone) with their attorneys at the end of the mediation before making a formal agreement. Other times, divorcing spouses choose to mediate before officially hiring an attorney. Mediators who are also attorneys—Attorney-Mediators—can also draft the legal documentation in some states.[14] The divorcing parents' attorneys also can draft the legal documentation or the parents can use the online forms if it they are available in the state.

Compared to litigation in divorce proceedings, mediation appears to have several benefits. An important study found that mediation helps to decrease conflict between parents after divorce, increase some aspects of positive co-parenting after divorce, and improve satisfaction with how the divorce was handled.[15] Other studies suggest that, compared to litigation, mediation is better at helping divorcing parents work through their anger, accept the loss of divorce, and attain some realistic hope regarding future relationships.[16] One very affluent couple we know used the divorce mediation process to divide up extensive property, develop a parenting plan, and decide on alimony and child support. The full range of issues was resolved in mediation so they could file uncontested paperwork through the courts. Although they had difficult circumstances, with the husband having a "girlfriend" waiting for the divorce process to finish, the mediation process helped to open up the communication lines for the couple to be effective in co-parenting their three children. Both spouses were able to feel that their many financial assets were fairly distributed and each was able to give input to one another about their needs and wants. The opportunity to be heard by the other spouse was especially needed in this case for the spouse who was still coping with the idea of being divorced. Because divorce mediation focuses on the future co-parenting relationship, they were able to see hope in their future as parents, since they would be tied together for the rest of their lives through the children. They were very satisfied with the mediation process because of the reduced time and cost, as well as the voice they had in making decisions.

E. What is collaborative law? How does it work in a divorce?

Collaborative law is where two attorneys are hired who are designated as "collaborative lawyers." Collaborative law is defined as "a legal process where the attorneys for the parties in a family dispute agree to assist them in resolving the conflict by using cooperative strategies rather than adversarial techniques and litigation. Early, non-adversarial participation by the attorneys allows them to use practices of good lawyering not often used in the usual adversarial proceedings, such as use of analysis and reasoning to solve problems, generation of options and creation of a positive context for settlement."[17] These collaborative lawyers have the divorcing spouses sign an agreement where they indicate they understand the attorneys are hired in order to come to an agreement outside of court or formal litigation. The attorneys work together with the divorcing spouses to try and come to a full agreement through negotiations.

Collaborative attorneys can usually be found by an online search. If the divorcing parents cannot agree on every issue, they will hire two new attorneys to go through the litigation process. This is rarely needed, however, as a well-known statistic shows that 96% of collaborative law cases settle outside of court.[18]

Not much research on collaborative law has been done yet. But one early investigation of divorcing parents who used collaborative law suggested that it may produce higher satisfaction with negotiations, more cooperation in negotiating, more creative solutions that meet family needs, and better communication between divorcing parents.[19] One prominent collaborative attorney[20] says that, "it has been my experience that, compared to court-ordered outcomes, the result in a collaborative divorce is more unique and personally tailored to the divorcing couple and their family. It will generally be more enduring and when modifications might be necessary, the parties have experienced a process that they can hopefully repeat in crafting changes without having to resort to court processes." States vary, however, in how much collaborative law is practiced.

F. What if I don't want the divorce? Can I challenge a divorce in court?

Although it takes two people to agree to marry, it only takes one person to divorce. Historically, the law required a major reason for divorce, such as insanity or adultery, but now the law only requires one person to assert that there are "irreconcilable differences" in the marriage.[21] In 2010, New York was the last state in the United States to pass a no-fault divorce law.[22] So every state in the United States now has no-fault divorce, which means you can divorce your spouse for any reason. Once one spouse insists on ending the marriage, it is futile for the other spouse to challenge the divorce in court. In this situation, there are legal limited options for the spouse who wants to save the marriage. A few states (Maine, Ohio, Pennsylvania, Utah) have a law that allows a spouse to go to a judge to request a brief "time out" in the divorce proceedings to allow for marriage counseling. But many lawyers are not even aware of these laws. In addition, three states (Arizona, Arkansas, Louisiana) have another way of entering into a marriage that some couples choose called "covenant marriage." Parties that enter into a covenant marriage have special requirements in order to divorce, such as getting counseling first, and the grounds for divorcing parents are limited to such things as abuse, addiction, adultery, abandonment, and imprisonment. Of course, many couples seek help to reconcile their marriage before divorcing by getting help from a marriage counselor.

Once the divorce is final, most states require that a person can make modifications only because of a "substantial change in circumstances."[23] Custody and parenting time can be modified through this substantial change in circumstances.[24] Assets and debts are rarely changed, but it is possible if a substantial change in circumstances is present.[25] Most states have rules regarding when child support can be modified. Alimony is usually harder to modify then child support. Some states require a substantial change "not foreseeable at the time of divorce" for modification of alimony.[26] Also, a person may feel that the court order is not in compliance with the actual law. In this case, the court order can be challenged through appeal within a specified amount of time after the divorce is final. Of course, these legal processes can be very costly. When a modification is needed, it is usually a good idea for people to try to use mediation before litigating with an attorney in court. Child support obligations cannot be avoided through bankruptcy.

Exercises for Chapter 8

8.1. Thinking About Parenting Time with Children.

One of the most important issues to settle in a divorce, if there are children involved, is how the children will allocate their time with each parent. It's important that parents try to decide this with the best interests of their children in mind rather than just considering their own wishes.

A. *Custody*. There are two types of custody: physical custody and legal custody.

Physical custody refers to where the children will reside. Visitation with the noncustodial parent where the other parent has sole physical custody is usually defined by state statute or through standards established by the majority of divorcing parents; it is most commonly every other weekend, mid-week visits, holiday visits, and extended time in the summer. Some states have a presumption in favor of joint physical custody.[27] For joint physical custody, the parents will share more overnights. Sometimes, people think that joint custody means 50-50 time. This is true for the most extreme joint custody, but there are also many other options for joint custody depending on your state standards. In Utah, for instance, any parent time that involves more than 111 overnights per year is considered joint custody. The most common joint custody arrangements involve a "fat weekend," which goes from Friday after school to the drop off on Monday morning at school and a mid-week overnight every other week or every week that begins after school, with drop off at school the next morning. Some parties chose to share the summer with each having 50%.

Legal custody refers to which parent will have access to records and make major decisions for the children concerning school, religion, and medical treatment. Most parents share joint legal custody, which means that both have access to records and work together to make major decisions for the children. Sole legal custody means that only one parent will make major decisions for the child.

Below, think about a possible responsibility and time-sharing plan that you feel would be in the best interests of your children and, as much as possible, fair to both parents. First, think about who will have custody of the children. Then, consider time-sharing during the school year and time-sharing when children are out of school, such as the summer months. Then think about time-sharing on special occasions, such as birthdays and holidays.

In the best interests of your children, who will have custody of the children, or will you share custody of the children? Why is this the best situation for your children? Write down your thoughts here:

_____

_____

_____

_____

_____

_____

_____

_____

B. *Time-Sharing Calendar—School Year.* On the calendar below, map out a possible time-sharing schedule for your children for those times of the year when they are in school.

SUN	MON	TUE	WED	THU	FRI	SAT
			1	2	3	4
5	6	7	8	9	10	11
12	13	14	15	16	17	18
19	20	21	22	23	24	25
26	27	28	29	30	31	

C. *Time-Sharing Calendar—Summer.* On the calendar below, map out a possible time-sharing schedule for your children for those times of the year when they are not in school.

SUN	MON	TUE	WED	THU	FRI	SAT
			1	2	3	4
5	6	7	8	9	10	11
12	13	14	15	16	17	18
19	20	21	22	23	24	25
26	27	28	29	30	31	

D. *Time Sharing on Special Occasions.* Sometimes it can be difficult to decide who will have the children on special occasions, such as birthdays and holidays. Below, make a list of possible special days and indicate how time with children will be shared or allocated on these occasions. Think of the best interests of your children.

Special Occasion (e.g., birthdays, holidays):	How could time with children be shared or allocated?

Chapter 8: What are the legal options for divorce?

8.2: Thinking About Child Support and Alimony

A. *Child Support*. How much money would you receive in child support? Go online and do a search for "[Your State] Child Support Calculator." Many states require different amounts of child support depending on the overnights that are spent with each parent.[28] Remember, child support is taxed to the person paying the support. Often the amount of child support awarded by the court is not the same as the amount expected and received.

Would you have enough to provide for yourself and your family? How would you supplement your income, if needed? What does this mean for your children as far as ample visitation? Write down your thoughts here:

_____

_____

_____

_____

_____

_____

_____

_____

B. *Alimony*. Alimony is rarely given in marriages of short duration and rarely goes for longer than the length of the marriage.[29] Alimony is taxed to the person who is receiving the support and is cannot be set aside in bankruptcy.[30] Men or women can pay alimony depending on which spouse is the higher wage earner and how much discrepancy there is in their incomes.[31] Some states have an alimony calculator, but the majority of states have no set guidelines for alimony. Some states have a statutory list, others standard of living, and some states have fault as a consideration for alimony.[32] Some states award alimony on an equalization basis to make sure each party has equal funds. Some states may consider an imputed income, which means that even if you are not working you may be counted as receiving the income you potentially could make for purposes of the alimony calculation. Other alimony standards are based on the parties' budgets and their earning capacities. Some people choose to go back to school after getting divorced and "rehabilitative alimony" may be appropriate. Rehabilitative alimony is a short-term alimony that helps a person get job training or schooling.

Review your answers on Exercise 7.1, "Thinking About the Financial Consequences of Divorce," or do the exercise now. After reviewing your budget, add together the expected amount of monthly income and the estimated child support paid or received. Is there a deficit? If so, how much? How will you make modifications in your budget to meet your finances? How do you feel about paying or receiving alimony? What would be a reasonable time frame? Write down your thoughts here:

_____

_____

_____

_____

_____

_____

_____

_____

8.3: Preparing for Divorce Mediation

The more thinking you do ahead of time about the issues you will need to settle in divorce mediation, the smoother things will go, the less time it will take, and the less it will cost. So, to help with this, answer the questions below as best you can.

Problem Definition	
What are main items for mediation from your perspective?	How do you think your spouse is defining the items for mediation?
	1.
1.	2.
2.	3.
3.	4.
4.	5.
5.	
	What are your goals for your children?
What are your goals for mediation?	1.
	2.
1.	3.
2.	
3.	
Option 1: Status Quo Continues	
What options are you considering if there are no changes in current temporary arrangement?	What options do you think the other side is considering if there are no changes in temporary arrangement?
1.	1.
2.	2.
3.	3.
4.	4.
5.	5.

Option 2: Listing Non-Negotiables (An item about which you are not willing to make any concessions.) What is non-negotiable for you?	What do you think is non-negotiable for your spouse?
Option 3: Creating New Options What options would make you satisfied? 1. 2. 3. 4. 5.	What options do you think would make your spouse satisfied? 1. 2. 3. 4. 5.
Option 4: Commitment to Process What are you willing to offer and make a commitment to?	How would you like to communicate with your ex-spouse if a future problem arises?
Option 5: Learning from the Past If you could go back in time what would you do differently? Why?	Are you willing to learn from the past problem and move forward? Are you willing to move forward with a cooperative co-parenting relationship?

Endnotes to Chapter 8

[1] See American Bar Association. (2013). A review in the year of family law, "Grounds for divorce and residency requirement." *Family Law Quarterly, 46,* 530–533.

[2] Pollet, S., & Lombreglia, M. (2008). A nationwide survey of mandatory parent education, *Family Courts Review, 46*(2), 375–394.

[3] See Utah Code Ann. § 30-3-32 to § 30-3-37; Utah Code Ann. § 30-3-5(1); Utah Code Ann. § 30-3-5(1); Utah Code Ann. § 30-3-5(8); Utah Code Ann. § 78-45-7.1–7.11.

[4] See Utah Code Ann. § 78-45-7.5(7).

[5] See American Bar Association. (2013). A review in the year of family law, "Child support guidelines." *Family Law Quarterly, 46*(4), 528–529.

[6] See Utah Code Ann. § 78-45-7.5(5)(b).

[7] An Affidavit of Impecuniosity can be filed for low-income parties. See Utah Code Ann. § 78-7-35 (Supp. 2006).

[8] See Utah Rules of Professional Conduct 1.7.

[9] See Utah Code Ann. § 78-31b-7(3) and Utah Rules of Professional Conduct 2.4(c).

[10] Texas Family Code §153.014.

[11] See Utah Code Ann. § 78-31b-2.

[12] See Utah Code Ann. § 78-31b-7(3).

[13] See Utah Code of Judicial Administration 4-510.

[14] See Utah Code Ann. § 78-31b-7(3) and Utah Rules of Professional Conduct 2.4(c).

[15] Emery, R. E., Laumann-Billings, L., Waldron, M., Sbarra, D. A., & Dillon, P. (2001). Child custody mediation and litigation: Custody, contact, and coparenting 12 years after initial dispute resolution. *Journal of Consulting and Clinical Psychology, 69,* 323–332; Sbarra, D. A., & Emery, R. E. (2008). Deeper into divorce: Using actor-partner analyses to explore difference in coparenting conflict following custody evaluation. *Journal of Family Psychology, 22,* 144–152, 144.

[16] Ackerman, M. J. (2001). *Clinician's guide to child custody evaluations, 2nd ed.* New York: John Wiley & Sons.

[17] Definition found on http://www.cflutah.org/about%20collaborative%20law.htm

[18] This is a well-known statistic in legal cases. See abanet.org and *GP Solo18*(4), June 2001.

[19] Macfarlane, J. (2005) *The emerging phenomenon of collaborative family law (CFL): A qualitative study of CFL cases.* Retrieved from http://canada.justice.gc.ca/eng/pi/pad-rpad/rep-rap/2005_1/2005_1.pdf

[20] Brian Florence is a prominent collaborative lawyer in Utah.

[21] See Utah Code Ann. § 30-3-1.

[22] See New York Domestic Relations Law § 170.

[23] Custody and parent time can be modified if there is a "substantial change in circumstances." See *Fullmer v. Fullmer,* 761 P.2d 942, 946 (Utah App. 1988) and Utah Code Ann. § 30-3-10.4. Assets and debts are rarely changed, yet the court could modify them if a substantial change has occurred. See Utah Code Ann. § 30-3-5(3) (Lexis Supp. 2007) and *Childs v. Callahan,* 993 P.2d 244, 247 (Utah App. 1999). To modify alimony, the court requires a substantial change "not foreseeable at the time of divorce." Utah Code Ann. § 30-3-5(8)(g)(ii)(Lexis Supp. 2007).

[24] See *Fullmer v. Fullmer,* 761 P.2d 942, 946 (Utah App. 1988) and Utah Code Ann. § 30-3-10.4.

[25] See Utah Code Ann. § 30-3-5(3) (Lexis Supp. 2007) and *Childs v. Callahan,* 993 P.2d 244, 247 (Utah App. 1999).

[26] Utah Code Ann. § 30-3-5(8)(g)(ii) (Lexis Supp. 2007).

[27] See American Bar Association. (2013). A review in the year of family law, "Custody criteria." *Family Law Quarterly, 46*(4), 524–527.

[28] See American Bar Association. (2013). A review in the year of family law, "Custody criteria." *Family Law Quarterly, 46*(4), 524–527.

[29] See Utah Code Ann. § 30-3-5(8)(h) (Lexis Supp. 2007).

[30] See 11 U.S.C.S. § 523(a)(5) (Lexis Supp. 2007) and 26 U.S.C. § 71(a) (2000).

[31] See Utah Code Ann. § 30-3-5(8)(a) (Lexis Supp. 2007). The seven factors for alimony are: (1) the financial condition and needs of the person who is to receive alimony, (2) the earning capacity of the person who is to receive alimony, (3) the ability of the person who is to pay alimony to provide support, (4) the length of the marriage, (5) whether or not the recipient spouse worked in a business that was owned or operated by the payor spouse, and (7) whether or not the recipient spouse directly contributed to an increase in the payor spouse's skill "by paying for education received by the payor spouse or allowing the payor spouse to attend school during the marriage."

[32] See American Bar Association. (2013). A review in the year of family law, "Alimony/Spousal support factors." *Family Law Quarterly, 46*(4), 522–523.

Resource List

Below are some possible resources that some people who have divorced, or who are thinking about divorce or reconciliation have found helpful. Although we do not endorse these organizations or their services, we believe that they can be helpful for many people.

Center for Divorce Education: www.divorce-education.com

National Family Resiliency Center: www.divorceabc.com

National Parents Organization: www.nationalparentsorganization.org

Association of Family and Conciliation Courts:
www.afccnet.org/resourcecenter/resourcesforfamilies

National Stepfamily Resource Center: www.stepfamilies.info

Reconciliation Resources (religious):

Retrouvaille: www.retrouvaille.org

Marriage 911 Ministry: www.reconciliationgodsway.com

A Summary of Key Points in this Guidebook

❖ This guidebook is designed for individuals and couples who are thinking about divorce. It includes research-based information and exercises to help them make the best decision going forward—to divorce or to keep trying to repair the marriage.

❖ Most states require that parents going through a divorce participate in a brief class to help them help their children adjust to divorce. A few states include consideration of the possibility of reconciliation in these classes.

❖ Divorce is both a personal and public issue. A national study estimated the annual cost of the breakdown of marriage in the United States to be $112 billion.

❖ Many unhappy marriages become happy again. At any one time, 10% of married individuals report that they are unhappy in their marriage. Five years later, 20% of unhappily married individuals have divorced, but 50% are still married and say they are now happy in their marriage; another 20% say their marriage has improved. Only 10% of unhappily married individuals are still married and unhappy 5 years later.

❖ Some people read books or use other resources to repair their marriages on their own. Others participate in marriage education classes that teach valuable relationship skills. Still others seek professional marriage counseling or guidance from a religious leader.

❖ 80% of couples show improvement after visiting a marriage counselor and up to 50% say that most of their major problems were resolved. But only about half of divorcing couples seek formal marriage counseling.

❖ About half of all divorces come from marriages that are not experiencing high levels of conflict; individuals from these marriages generally experience a decrease in happiness over time. When individuals end high-conflict marriages, however, they increase their happiness, on average. About two in ten individuals appear to enhance their lives through their divorce, but about three in ten seem to do worse after divorce; about four in ten individuals build future romantic relationships after divorce but they have mostly the same kinds of problems as they did in their previous marriage.

❖ A significant minority (about 25%) of divorced individuals say they have regrets about their divorce.

- About three out of four divorced people will eventually remarry someone else. However, second marriages have even higher rates of divorce, although if couples can hang on through the challenging first 5 years of remarriage, their chances for success are high.

- 40%–50% of first marriages end in divorce; about 60% of second marriages end in divorce. The most common reasons that individuals give for their divorce are lack of commitment, too many arguments, infidelity, marrying too young, unrealistic expectations, and a lack of equality. However, about half of divorces come from low-conflict marriages; these divorces are hardest on the children.

- The challenges of divorce can have negative consequences on children's social, emotional, intellectual, physical, moral, and spiritual development. Research suggests that children who experience divorce are generally at two to three times the risk for various problems. However, many children are resilient; even though the experience can be painful, most do not experience serious long-term problems from divorce.

- Children caught in high-conflict marriages generally do better if their parents divorce, compared to children who remain in high-conflict marriages. But children in low-conflict marriages generally do worse when their parents divorce compared to children who remain in low-conflict marriages.

- In adulthood, children who experienced the divorce of their parents are two to three times more likely to divorce, compared to children who did not experience the divorce of their parents.

- Compared to adults in a stable marriage, divorced adults, on average, have poorer physical and mental health.

- A few years after divorce, a large majority of divorced fathers no longer have regular contact with their children.

- Researchers estimate that divorcing individuals would need more than a 30% increase in income, on average, to maintain the same standard of living they had prior to their divorce.

- About one in five women fall into poverty as a result of divorce. Three out of four divorced mothers don't receive full payment of child support.

- Most men also experience a loss in their financial well-being after a divorce, a loss generally of about 10%–40%, depending on their circumstances.

- Divorce law varies from state to state in the United States. The divorce process can take anywhere from one month to several years.

- ❖ Some states have a waiting period for the divorce to be completed.
- ❖ Mediation is a process where a trained, neutral professional will try to help couples reach agreements about issues related to their divorce.
- ❖ Every state in the United States has "no fault" divorce. Therefore, even though one spouse may not want the divorce, the divorce will be granted.

About the Authors

Dr. Alan J. Hawkins, Ph.D., has been a member of the faculty in the School of Family Life at Brigham Young University since 1990. He is the former chair of the Utah Marriage Commission. He also serves on the Research Advisory Group for the Oklahoma Marriage Initiative. He helps teach the required divorce orientation education class for divorcing parents in Utah. He has published dozens of scholarly articles and several books on marriage, divorce, and fathering.

Dr. Tamara A. Fackrell, J.D., Ph.D., is an Attorney Mediator in Utah. She has had a private mediation practice focusing on divorce and domestic mediation since 1997 and a private law practice since 1998 focusing on family law. She earned her Ph.D. in Marriage, Family, and Human Development from Brigham Young University in 2012. Previously, she graduated cum laude from the BYU Law School. Dr. Fackrell is a Master Mediator and Primary Trainer for the State of Utah and performs certifications in mediation and divorce mediation for professionals.

Dr. Steven M. Harris, Ph.D., LMFT, is a Professor and Director of the Couple and Family Therapy Program at the University of Minnesota. He also serves as the Associate Director of the Minnesota Couples on the Brink Project. He has served as both a member and the Chair of the Texas Healthy Marriage Initiative's Research Advisory Group and is currently an active member of the Oklahoma Marriage Initiative's Research Advisory Group. He publishes and presents regularly on topics related to the practice of marital therapy and discernment counseling.

The authors express their gratitude to many individuals who allowed us to interview them about their personal experiences at the crossroads of divorce. We changed their names and sometimes a few details of their stories to respect their privacy. In addition, we are grateful for the many research assistants for their work on developing this guidebook, including Carma Martino Needham, Brittanie Beeson, Fawn Bennion, Victoria Blanchard, Elise Burnett, Shayne Dickson, Marissa Dittmore, Kimberlee Earl, Elizabeth Fawcett, Kristin Fixmer, Karalynn Forrest, Walter Hartje, Scott Huff, Alan Larson, Chelsey Long, Emily Luschin, Monica Mays, Sarah Pierce, Alexis Rasmussen, Heidi Reid, Valene Rose, Rebecca Score, Rachael Shaw, Cristina Smith, Elizabeth Van Patten, and Courtney Welling.